RE-IMAGINING EDUCATION

ESSAYS ON REVIVING THE SOUL OF LEARNING

edited by
Dennis Patrick Slattery
and
Jennifer Leigh Selig

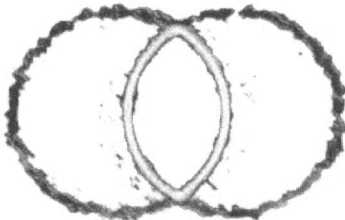

MANDORLA BOOKS

ISBN: 978-1-950186-05-1

Previously released by Spring Publications (2009)

Designed by Jennifer Leigh Selig

Cover art by Tallmadge Doyle
"Homage to Giordano Bruno VII"
www.tallmadgedoyle.com
Used with permission.

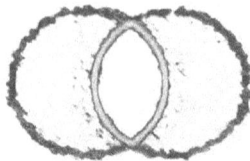

MANDORLA BOOKS
WWW.MANDORLABOOKS.COM

The need for imagination, as a sense of truth, and as a feeling of responsibility — these are the three forces which are the very nerve of education.

~Rudolf Steiner

The best education is not given to students; it is drawn out of them.

~Gerald Belcher

I entered the classroom with the conviction that it was crucial for me and every other student to be an active participant, not a passive consumer. . . education that connects the will to know with the will to become.

~ bell hooks

TABLE OF CONTENTS

Preface to the 2019 Edition (Dennis Patrick Slattery).................. vii

Foreword (Dennis Patrick Slattery)... ix

Introduction (Jennifer Leigh Selig) xvii

City, Soul and Myth (James Hillman)..3

The Dance of Learning (Thomas Moore) 9

Chronos vs. Kairos: A Plea for the Restoration of Empathy and
Imagination in History Teaching (Ruth Meyer)............................19

Good Teaching Doesn't Count! (David L. Miller).............................31

Finding the Philosopher's Stone (Robin L. Gordon)..........................41

Restoring Soul to Teaching: Reflections on the Division of Spirit from
Matter in Teaching and Learning (Betty J. McEady)........................53

"Trying to Touch What Matters": Confessions of a High School Dropout
(Jennifer Leigh Selig) 69

Soul-Centered Education: An Interview with Stephen Aizenstat (Nancy
Treadway Galindo) 79

What White Whale Breaches? Classroom as Sacred Space (Dennis Patrick
Slattery) 89

Spiritual Resonance in the Classroom (Christipher M. Bache) 99

Poetic Awareness: Imagining and the Experience of Soul (Matthew Green)
....109

"Till We Have Faces": Image of Psyche (Elizabeth Fergus-Jean)..............121

Teaching Thinking (Edward S. Casey)...133

The Eros of Teaching (Christine Downing) 145

The Authority of the Teacher (Claudia Allums)............................151

Teaching Joseph Campbell and the Arthurian Romance (Evans Lansing
Smith)..159

Under the Helmet (Mary Aswell Doll)...169

Teaching as Mothering the Soul (Rosemarie Anderson) 177

Contributor Biographies 187

PREFACE TO THE 2019 EDITION

Dennis Patrick Slattery

As coeditor with Jennifer Leigh Selig, I am delighted to write a brief preface for the second edition of *Reimagining Education: Essays on Reviving the Soul of Learning,* formerly published by Spring Publications (2009). Ten years have passed since its initial debut and the essays within are even more relevant today when I sense at times that humanity has lost its bearings and is experiencing a drift into homelessness in the cosmos. Learning within the vessel of the humanities can help us to counter this drift by anchoring the imagination more broadly within the fields comprised by the humanities. Just as importantly, what links both teacher and student in such a rich cooperative is the force field of vocation.

A few days ago, while driving home, I listened to a radio station in which a professional man railed against the irresponsibility of those parents who allowed their children to study on the college level subjects that they were called to, that they had a passion for, but that did not necessarily lead them in a straight line to employment once they earned their degree. "How stupid, how irresponsible are these kids' parents," he sputtered, outraged. "Any education that does not lead to employment is a waste of time." Job acquisition was, for him, the only reason to continue one's learning. Of course, there is a certain truth in this claim, but what saddened me most was the absolute reduction of learning to earning. Discussion of purpose, satisfaction, or the soul's fulfillment in his narrow vision of education was not even hinted at. The imagination was discounted as of no account. The myths of utility and economics had eclipsed all other considerations.

I contrast the moralistic stance above with an observation or two from the psychologist C. G. Jung on the miracle of vocation, which he refers to as "an irrational factor that destines a man to emancipate himself from the herd and its well-worn paths. True personality is always a vocation and puts its trust in it as in God, despite its being, as the ordinary man would say, only a personal feeling" (*CW* 17, par. 300).[1] To be called to a destiny, to hear such a voice and to heed it is what the mythologist Joseph Campbell referred to as "the initial conditions for the hero's journey" (*The Hero With a Thousand Faces*, 53).[2] The essays in this volume each speak, whether directly or indirectly, to the teacher's role in aiding one's students in such a calling. What could be more important than having the destiny of another in one's purview to help nurture on the road to its individuation?

C. G. Jung in the same essay addresses the professional whose story I began with: "In the place of the inner voice there is the voice of the group with its conventions, and vocation is replaced by collective necessities. But even in this unconscious social condition there are not a few who are *called awake* by the summons of the voice, whereupon they are at once set apart from the others, . . ." (par. 302, my emphasis).[3]

One of the most important roles of teachers whose voices resonate with the soul of learning, is to stimulate and encourage this call to awakening, which alone is the central impetus of the soul to realize itself through its learning. Then indeed a revival has begun. We hope this persuasive and soulful collection of voices will revive your own interest in and love of learning.

Notes

[1] C.G. Jung. *The Development of Personality: Papers on Child Psychology, Education, and Related Subjects.* Volume 15 of the Collected Works of C.G. Jung. Bollingen Series XX. Trans. By R.F.C Hull. Princeton: Princeton University Press, 1981.

[2] Joseph Campbell, *The Hero With a Thousand Faces.* Bollingen Series XVII. Princeton: Princeton University Press, 2004.

[3] C.G. Jung. *The Development of Personality: Papers on Child Psychology, Education, and Related Subjects.* Volume 15 of the Collected Works of C.G. Jung. Bollingen Series XX. Trans. By R.F.C Hull. Princeton: Princeton University Press, 1981.

FOREWORD

Dennis Patrick Slattery

Socrates and saints teach by existing.
~George Steiner[1]

There occurs a scene, early in Book One of Homer's *Odyssey*,[2] when the goddess Athena, born, you remember, fully formed from the consciousness of Zeus, her father, suddenly appears very quietly in the hall of Odysseus' palace in the twentieth year of his absence. In the din created by the reckless suitors, no one but Odysseus' son, Telemachos, even notices her. She is in disguise as Mentes. Her wisdom includes not appearing in her full and spectacular essence, for it would be too much reality for mortals to absorb. From Mentes we derive the words *mind, mentor* and *mental,* even *mindfulness.* She is, in this divine instant, the presence of, or the occasion of, the moment of learning, sacredly inspired and supremely timed, for learning involves, among other elements, the art of timing—of *kairos* itself. She is also the presence of learning that is mindful, not rote, of knowledge that attends the presence of wisdom, not information, of understanding, not data processing. She is, in her disguise, the quality of learning itself. Under her tutelage one's language itself is transformed.

Having all the time in the world, she waits patiently, at the threshold, noticing, fully aware of what she has just stepped into: the chaotic classroom where no learning is possible because of the absence of piety. But this virtue is not completely absent. Piety in the guise of hospitality mandates that the guest be noticed and then treated according to its indomitable code, which is a kind of foundational behavior of a civilized household and, by extension, a virtuous city. The epic suggests that to be mindful is to be hospitable. In such a terrain learning has the opportunity to take deep root and blossom. In learning, both guest and host, student and teacher, participate in a common heritage.

Alluded to above, the only person to approach her in the chaotic and consuming behavior of the suitors who are there to win Penelope's hand is the young Telemachos. He treats the stranger with great respect: he finds a seat for her, offers her food, and invites her into a still center of conversation amidst the surrounding chaos. His behavior indicates that he is disposed to learning because of the largesse he shows this stranger. His heart is generous.

Mentes, in exchange, has nothing to offer the young host but her words, carriers of divine wisdom, so she instructs him not only in how the son of Odysseus is to begin his education, but she also inspires him. She does so by breathing into the young man a divine knowing, *in spiritus,* which is represented most emphatically by the way Telemachos' speech alters dramatically as a consequence of such a profound encounter with wisdom, divinely transported. Not just his vocabulary but his voice changes; he has, as a result of his encounter with Mentes, gained in both authority and force of presence, which surprises himself as much as it does the suitors, cowards all, as well as it does the servants in the hall.

For the first time in his young life, Telemachos speaks with the voice of a presence beyond himself. When he opens his mouth to reprimand the suitors for their absence of all moderation in appetite and for their worship of always-consuming insatiable bellies, witness to a sustained absence of respect for the gods, they stop chewing in mid-mouthful, look at him startled, then gaze at one another in both consternation and fear. They recognize for the first time that authority now accompanies his speech. Even as they retain the power that comes with numbers, the young man now carries within himself the force of divine presence. Slaying him is their only recourse to escape his possible influence, the suitors believe, out of their newly-acquired fear of his presence. Divinity has entered the act of learning.

This brief story in one of the great poems of world literature about the disposition of the soul to learn was at one time expelled from the house of education as an unwelcome guest. Now reinstated in many curricula, the story constitutes one of the inspirations for this volume, composed by teachers, each of whom has taught in various capacities for at least fifteen years. The hope is that their stories, insights, and experiences in the classroom can serve to invite Mentes, in the form of the mythic goddess Athena, back into the imagination of learning and to the learning instinct endemic to the soul.

For over 12 years, I have taught teachers the classics at both The Dallas Institute of Humanities and Culture and The Fairhope Institute of Humanities and Culture in Fairhope, Alabama. The Dallas program was designed in 1983 by Dr. Louise Cowan, The Fairhope program by the present director of the Dallas Institute, Dr. Larry Allums. During those summers I learned of the frustrations, the discouragements, as well as the small candles of light that gave teachers hope in a system that continued to beat them down, up—and often—out of the profession. Sluggish bureaucrats were replacing the sparking enthusiasms evoked by teachers in the classroom. Teachers' discouragement was often assuaged by their becoming learners again in the summer programs, where for two consecutive years they studied the classics, argued with one another, and became tribal and intimate in their conversations. There they shared their frustrations over a system more concerned with accountability measured by numerical mine fields of test results than in shapes of wonder passing across students' faces as they excitedly engaged in learning.

In one of the Dallas Institute's *Newsletters* occasioned by the Teachers' Institute, Louise Cowan writes of the teacher's role in countering the quantitative and objectivistic impulse of education management today:

> But a teacher is not a mere guide in crafts or techniques, nor even simply a stimulator of thought, important as those functions may be. The teacher is a mediator, a conductor, between one world and another, between ignorance and comprehension, in the way that Athena guides Odysseus and Vergil guides Dante.[3]

How different is her image of the teacher from the individual in the classroom assaulted by lesson plans, teaching to the test, struggling to meet mandates that ensure school funding, and creating behavioral objectives under the skinny, even anemic, mythos of science and mathematical measurement.

In a recent article in *The Chronicle of Higher Education*, a year after Secretary of Education Margaret Spellings initiated a commission to discover more encompassing ways to measure accountability in both lower and higher education, the Commission called on higher education "to shed some of its mystery and fundamentally prove the value it delivers."[4]

The article went on to cite the commission's intention, namely,

> ...devising new measures that allow comparisons of student performances. That means developing standardized tests and compiling and sharing more data on both "inputs" and "outcomes," including total student costs and college completion rates.[5]

Two observations are worth citing here. In his devastating article, "Schoolhouse Crock: Fifty Years of Blaming America's Educational System for Our Stupidity," Peter Schrag surveys the last half-century of American educational reforms. There he quotes former Secretary of Education Charles Finn, under the Reagan Administration, who claims that many of the "touted reforms" were "irrelevant, and probably harmful."[6] On accountability measures, Schrag himself believes, "What makes the likelihood of success, and the measurement of outcomes, even less certain is that these reforms tend to come in cycles of contradictory trends."[7] One such contradiction, he recounts, was a rush to catch up with the Russian Sputnik surprise and soon thereafter a shift to attend to poor and minority children.[8] The contradiction inherent here was to push hard the science and math students at the top of their classes to excel in these disciplines while at the same time increase the scores of the underachiever. The goals of the two impulses split the energy of education into both excelling and remediating.

It seems, in reading this article, which offers a wide survey of differing points of view on how to "fix" American education, that the tail of accountability has been wagging the dog of learning at great expense and with questionable results. We who are focused on the art of teaching are presented yet another bone to gnaw on as a fix for failed pedagogy and measurement standards. Clearly, measurement as myth is not a method for success. So accountability itself might best be held accountable. Our own thinking is that accountability measures are in fact witness to a failure of imagination, both in learning and in efficacy in America's schools.

Absent from the discussion, which makes the national conversation on education often sclerotic, are words like: imagination, transformation, discernment, fullness of vision, self-knowledge, inquiry, wonder, and ripening. Absent as well is a vision of teacher as more than a test-preparer and administrator. Presented as virtue is the myth of measurement and its stepchild, accountability. Now this language smacks of "being responsible," which on the surface appears as a virtue. But what does it insist on? That what is learned can be measured and in fact must be measurable, otherwise it has little value. In other words, teach what can be measured, for only such accountability can prove that learning is occurring. Any supersensible change in the soul of a learner who sneezes at measurement is deemed unworthy of the enterprise of learning.

By contrast, Parker Palmer writes in *To Know as We are Known* that the role of learning is "the formation of the spirit" of a student, a practice that rests securely on a philosophic ground, not a behavioral stimulus-response ideology.[9] Palmer adumbrates the role of learning not as acquisition of information but closer to a spiritual process within a community.[10] He senses a certain transparency in the act of both teaching and learning "whose end is not explanation but contemplation."[11]

Louise Cowan's vision is more expansive, even epic in its thrust: "The schools exist to implant within the young the most valued knowledge of a culture, its treasured ideals. These cannot be transmitted by indoctrination but only that that magical power—liberal education—which preserves individual freedom as it leads a student onward."[12] One could in contemplating Dr. Cowan's words grow cynical about the elimination, even the expulsion, of freedom in today's education, which appears to prefer instead to produce work drones bent on consuming, as an unworthy substitute for what is missing in their lives: a sense of the mythic, spiritual wisdom of traditions.

Emphasizing, rather, the mystery of teaching, the literary and cultural critic George Steiner reflects on more than fifty years in the classroom. He reminds us of the calling, the vocative quality of teaching, of its "summons" that calls the authentic teacher: "The teacher is aware of the magnitude and, if you will, the mystery of his profession, of that which he has professed in an unspoken Hippocratic oath."[13] Both authentic and substantial teaching and learning are erotic, memorial, mysterious, and full of the musings that Mnemosyne, Mother of the Muses, offers to those who engage the Eros of the classroom, or of any setting where learning is invited, untrammeled, to take place. The idea that "teaching and learning are informed by an otherwise inexpressible sexuality of the human soul" intrigues.[14] Eros finds a corridor in the dialogue between teaching and learning that is reciprocal, repetitive, and renewing.

The current lexicon that debases and objectifies these qualities depletes the energy engaged in the creativity of teaching and learning; it seeks to objectify, demystify, and degrade the erotics of Memory that must be present in the engagement, if not in the full-blown marriage, of the teacher and learner. The American poet William Stafford offers in "A Message from the Wanderer" the kind of engaged retrieval that can enrich so beautifully the joy of learning:

> Thus freedom always came nibbling my thought,
> just as—often, in light, on the open hills—
> you can pass an antelope and not know
> and look back, and then—even before you see—
> there is something wrong about the grass.
> And then you see.[15]

Such seeing can, of course, occur singly, in a private experience that Stafford invites us to join; it most often occurs, as the essays in this volume reveal, in *communitas*, in a communal mingling of related but distinct students. Louise Cowan, borrowing the term from Victor Turner, who made it popular in his writing on ritual, describes *communitas* an occasion when

> a group of people assemble for a creative purpose, their energy and desire welding them—if only temporarily—into a unity. A certain atmosphere of ceremony prevails, with a sense of liminality—of being on a threshold, at a turning point of some significance marking a change in the direction of one's life.[16]

They are asked, she goes on, to step out of their worlds in order to "participate in a ritual gathering, in which, as a group, with guidance, they explore the meaning of what Turner speaks of as 'archaic symbols.'"[17] These moments are in large measure what the various teachers who contribute to this volume are expressing, however mysterious they are to delineate.

Although the collection of essays, at once theoretical and practical in scope and intention, is historically tethered to a moment in time, one that witnesses a crisis in learning, our intention is not to link the essays in a reactionary way but to see the present as occasion to retrieve, renew, and revision the enchantment of learning. One might ask: what timeless and perennial qualities of excellence are germane to teaching and learning insofar as they both serve the life of imagination and the further cultivation of the soul? The answer rests in the essays themselves as repositories by teachers with decades of experience in the classroom faced with administrative directives that discouraged some and encouraged others. We let them speak their own truths that have informed thousands of learners young and old.

We hope that such a volume, with differing frames, varied language, fresh stories, and new insights, will reinvigorate learning with its intrinsic joy and wonder. We are proud of the variety of experiences, teaching levels, and passions of the teachers in this volume.

Notes

1 George Steiner, *Lessons of the Masters: The Charles Eliot Norton Lectures, 2001–2002,* vol. 4 (Cambridge: Harvard University Press, 2003).

2 Homer, *The Odyssey,* trans. and ed. Albert Cook (New York: Norton, 1967).

3 Louise Cowan, *The Dallas Institute Newsletter,* ed. Donald and Louise Cowan (Dallas: The Dallas Institute Publications, 1992), 10–11.

4 Paul Basken, "A Year Later, Spellings Report Still Makes Ripples," *The Chronicle of Higher Education* 14, no. 5 (September 28, 2007): 1–12.

5 Ibid., A–20.

6 Peter Schrag, "Schoolhouse Crock: Fifty Years of Blaming America's Educational System for Our Stupidity," *Harper's,* September 2007, 38.

7 Ibid., 41.

8 Ibid.

9 Parker Palmer, *To Know as We are Known: Education as a Spiritual Journey* (San Francisco, CA. HarperCollins, 1993), 13.

10 Ibid., 18.

11 Ibid.

12 Cowan, *Newsletter,* 11.

13 Steiner, *Lessons of the Masters,* 17.

14 Ibid., 17.

15 William Stafford, "A Message from the Wanderer," in *The Way It Is: New and Selected Poems* (St. Paul, MN: Greywolf Press, 1998), 53.

16 Cowan, "The Literary Mode of Knowing," *Classic Texts and the Nature of Authority,* 15.

17 Ibid.

INTRODUCTION

Jennifer Leigh Selig

When my colleague Dennis Patrick Slattery and I first hatched the plan for this volume, we sat down to write letters of invitation to our contributors, giving them very little direction. "Share with us any important insights you have gleaned from teaching and learning in your fifteen-plus years of teaching," we suggested. Write "a memoir, a reminiscence, or a reverie on teaching's more imaginal geography as you have both discovered and created it in your students over the years." We explained, "The general intention of the volume is for each participant to reveal a language that captures the soul of his or her own teaching through instructing, guiding, or inspiring students."

I must admit to being a bit nervous when we sent out the invitations. What if all eighteen essays were repetitious, more reiterative than creative? After all, Dennis and I were sending the invitation to teachers we knew, many of whom shared our affiliation with Pacifica Graduate Institute, a small but flourishing private university in California with an educational mission of "tending soul in and of the world." Dennis teaches there in the Mythological Studies Department, I teach in the Depth Psychology Department, and some of our contributors were either students or teachers there too, or were, by virtue of our association with them, merely one degree of separation away from Pacifica. Would we, as editors, be choir leaders for soul, with our singers all intoning the same note?

I worried, too, about the opposite: What if the eighteen essays were so disparate that they shared nothing in common? After all, though many of us had a common connection to Pacifica and/or to each other, as well as a commitment to ensouled education, the similarities stopped there. The teachers we invited into this volume spanned different ages (from their forties to their eighties), different disciplines (from philosophy to English to history to mythological studies to science and more), different educational venues (from public schools to private schools to workshops, institutes, and home schools), have taught different age groups (from elementary school to university to adult education), and have filled different responsibilities within education (from principals to school presidents to teacher educators). Given such diversity, would we find enough commonalities to hold a volume together? Were we, as editors, courting cacophony rather than symphony?

Dennis, the more experienced writer and editor that he is and, moreover, a true mentor of mine, just smiled and with Zen-like wisdom suggested, "Let's just see what happens." And he was right. I shouldn't have worried, I discovered later when all eighteen essays were sitting in front of me. *E pluribus unum.* Out of many, one. One soul, with many expressions. One volume, with many voices.

When in one weekend I read all the essays together, looking for an arrangement, I saw many harmonic lines connecting them even as each stands alone. James Hillman's essay, "City, Soul, and Myth," became the obvious place to begin. Though Hillman's topic in this essay is psychoanalysis, we can easily substitute the word "education" for psychoanalysis and ask ourselves his question, "Is education a work of civilization or of culture?" Hillman's distinction between the two allows us to see into the heart of the tension in modern education, a tension between those who believe the goal of education is to civilize our students and those who believe the goal should be instead to provide them with an experience of culture. Although no one argues against the civilizing function of education, the contributors in this volume make their various passionate pleas for the classroom as a place of culture, as a true school for the soul.

In his essay Hillman contrasts one of the Greek gods of civilization, Athene, with three gods of culture, Dionysus, Poseidon, and Aphrodite. Other contributors to this volume evoke different gods and different myths of education as well. Thomas Moore in his essay "The Dance of Learning" writes of the Saturnian nature of modern education and uses the myth of Apollo and Daphne to illustrate how sometimes our students wish to elude our control. In "Teaching Joseph Campbell and the Arthurian Romance," Evans Lansing Smith traces his own hero's journey into and through education as inspired by his teacher Joseph Campbell, using the Grail quest as his defining myth. Ruth Meyer, in her essay "Chronos versus Kairos: A Plea for the Restoration of Empathy and Imagination in History Teaching," turns to the Muses for inspiration in the teaching of history. And, of course, Dennis Patrick Slattery writes in the Preface of the relationship between Telemachos and Mentes in *The Odyssey*.

Not only myths but metaphors mark many pages of this volume. Teacher is a metaphor for mother in Rosemarie Anderson's essay, "Teaching as Mothering the Soul," because "teachers mother what is possible in others." The metaphor of teacher as alchemist is the theme of the essay "Finding the Philosopher's Stone" by Robin Gordon. "Like the alchemists practicing their art," she writes, "I have found teaching to be a spiritual exercise or, more accurately, a reflection of my own soul work." In David Miller's essay "Good Teaching Doesn't Count!" he too compares education to alchemy and then to baseball. People who call for outcomes assessment, he argues, "don't understand the nature of the game." Thomas Moore also uses the metaphor of play in his essay, though his title "The Dance of Learning" suggests his central metaphor as he alternately describes learning as a tango, a waltz and, in its darker moments, a tarantella marked by a certain "Sadeian enterprise" between teacher and student. Other darker metaphors include the modern school as concentration camp (Ruth Meyer) and as paradise lost, explored in Betty McEady's essay "Restoring Soul to Teaching: Reflections on the Division of Spirit from Matter in Teaching and Learning."

Our writers illustrate Thomas Moore's contention that "education is never an objective enterprise; it is always colored by a strong fantasy about it." Beginning with Dennis Patrick Slattery's Preface and threading through the volume is an acknowledgment and critique of the current fantasy of education: that of accountability through standardization. David Miller's essay takes on the accountability fantasy most directly in "Good Teaching Doesn't Count!" Other contributors such as Betty McEady, Ruth Meyer, and Robin Gordon echo his critique, writing directly of the disheartening, mind-numbing, and soul-deadening effects of teaching in an educational system in which only test scores matter. This is also the theme of my essay, "'Trying to Touch What Matters': Confessions of a High School Dropout," in which I write about the changes in education that led me to drop out of teaching high school after sixteen years. I shared, "Ultimately, I quit teaching high school because I did not want to teach (only) what can be counted. I wanted to be un-accountable. This didn't mean I wanted to leave students behind, but rather it meant that I simply couldn't see students as mere accounts received. They were beautiful, unique, individual souls, and I did not want to see them standardized. I wanted them all to take something different from my classes, something that mattered to them, in the same way that I wanted to bring something different to my classes, something that mattered to me."

All of our contributors grapple with the question of what matters in the educational enterprise, though their varying backgrounds and experiences lead them to suggest different answers. For Edward S. Casey, with his background in philosophy, what matters most is teaching students to think and, what's more, to think about their thinking. In "Teaching Thinking," Casey argues for true teaching that, rather than giving students the thoughts of the teacher as an already-formed product, instead teaches students "the process of thinking itself." In "The Eros of Teaching," Christine Downing agrees that we should be teaching thinking, but she adds something else that matters: "I guess I want to encourage [students] to *love* . . ., for I would wish they might come to love thinking and to discover that one can think with one's whole being!"

Downing shares how she entered the vocation of teaching almost by accident, through her own love of learning. In contrast, Claudia Allums writes of being called to the profession since she was a child. She charts the progression of her fantasy of teaching from that of correcting students' ignorance to getting students to like her, then finally to guiding and mentoring students as they engage in the big ideas, or what she refers to as "forms." In "The Authority of the Teacher," Allums shares her journey toward what matters as she discovers what ennobles the profession. Mary Aswell Doll writes about her own journey in "Under the Helmet," describing how coming into her cronehood as an educator has shown her that "wisdom cannot be taught but that offering an experience can be mind-changing." What matters to her is that students find their authentic selves.

Other experiences that matter are explored by Matthew Green and Elizabeth Fergus-Jean. In "Poetic Awareness: Imagining and the Experience of Soul," Green describes leading his American students through the landscape of France, hoping they'll experience poetic awareness: "the capacity to engage the world with the heart." For Fergus-Jean, with her background in visual art, her essay "Till We Have Faces: Image as Psyche" argues that teaching an awareness of image matters: "It is the image 'which has lain at the center of one's soul' that I believe as teachers . . . we must try to bring to the surface. Then we can assist students in discovering ways in which they may dive into their own depths to see anew."

When those depths are plumbed and soul's treasures are brought to the surface, the classroom is a magical place, a sacred space, as many of our contributors illustrate. Evoked by questions from Nancy Galindo in "Soul-Centered Education," Stephen Aizenstat describes in rich detail what a soul-centered classroom looks like, feels like, even sounds like, and he sounds the clarion call for a return to the primacy of imagination in education. Dennis Patrick Slattery echoes Stephen Aizenstat's appreciation for the primacy of imagination, stating, "With the right temperature, the right care, the right nurturing, and sustained vigilance, the imagination as cultural organ ripens into new insights, interpretations, and meanings. Such is the magic membrane of a classroom that nourishes the soul of knowledge." His essay "What White Whale Breaches? Classroom as Sacred Space" focuses on the sacred magic that occurs when text, teacher, and students ignite the "admixture of myth, memory, and meaning," and suggests that wisdom emerges "when these varied and yet united forces of psychic energy coalesce in a common conversation." Christopher Bache's essay "Spiritual Resonance in the Classroom" explores those "elevated conversations" as well, those magical moments when he and his students "tapped into levels of creativity beyond our separate capacities."

We hope Bache's statement applies to this volume of essays as well, that readers will experience it as a series of "elevated conversations" by individual mentor teachers that tap "into levels of creativity beyond our separate capacities." We hope, following Hillman's distinction, that this book itself is not a work of civilization but one of culture. Hillman writes, "Civilization gets the job done as well and reasonably as possible. Culture is song; the song that breaks out in the midst of the job." This volume is intended to be a tribute to the song of education that breaks out when imagination and soul are present.

We hope it sings to you, whether teacher experienced or inexperienced, whether administrator, parent, or student yourself, whether you're in the choir of advocates for soul-centered education or a skeptic on the sidelines, not sure our song line is in concert with yours. Though it is easy to find much to despair about in education today, we have hope, and as Emily Dickinson wrote,

'Hope' is the thing with feathers
That perches in the soul
And sings the tune—
Without the words
And never stops at all.[1]

And now, on to the songs . . .

Notes

[1] Emily Dickinson, "'Hope' is the thing with feathers" in *The Complete Poems of Emily Dickinson*, ed. T. H. Johnson (Boston: Little, Brown and Company, 1951), 116.

RE-IMAGINING EDUCATION

CITY, SOUL AND MYTH

James Hillman

What is a civilized city? What do we mean by "civilization"? I have turned to my own profession to find a reply, for I have asked myself and my colleagues: is psychoanalysis a work of civilization or of culture? By becoming more civilized—tamed, mannered, adapted, and participatory—do we therefore become more cultured? If civilization requires cohesive structures of architecture, engineering, law, government, education, finance, supply and distribution—in short, bureaucracies of maintenance—to name but a few of the institutions that support civilization and are essential to cities, where does culture figure in, if at all? A city can be imagined, constructed, and can function efficiently, and progressively improve its functioning without theaters and music, think tanks, artists' quarters, red-light districts, stray dogs, and sparrows, without a helter-skelter variety of eateries, street vendopubs, without celebrations and commemorations, even without controversial newspapers and multiple radio stations.

Culture and its ferment may be a desirable accessory, but is it necessary to civilized order and security? Moreover, should places and budgets for culture be provided in urban planning? Such provisions may as well stifle culture as promote it. Culture seems to be beyond the rational control of civilization.

I have come to the conclusion that the work of psychoanalysis is one of culture because we have given up the addiction to the progress myth and adaptation to the institutions and conformities that civilization rightly demands. Our work with

3

soul tends to follow the *resistances* to civilization, those symptoms of inadaptability—depression, breakdown, outrage, panic, idiosyncratic peculiarities that have drawn the patient deeper into questions of fate, love, death, purpose, questions of soul that seem so often at odds with the requirements of civilization. "What's madness," asks the poet Theodore Roethke, "but nobility of soul at odds with circumstance."

II

There is a mythical component within these contrasting impulses of civilization and culture. A look over the shoulder at the model *polis* of the historical imagination with its protective Goddess, Athene, shows the contrasting myths at work.

Athene has been summoned up as "protectress of the civic order" and source of the idea of rational progress.[1] Many of her images present her dressed in defensive armor, shielded, helmeted, weaponed, with a small figure of victory on her shoulder. She guided the city magistrates and the city's generals with grey-eyed sober counseling. She was called a fortress, expressed by the militant defensiveness of a city's spirit, and the renewal of that spirit in victory: compare the team of Liverpool over Chelsea, over Milan! (In fact, and just by the way, the melting pot integration of the disparate populations of the bulging American cities at the turn of the twentieth century was enabled by the whole city's identification with its baseball team and the public democracy of the local stadium.)

Athene also gave intelligence, reflection, wise decision-making to leaders such as Ulysses,[2] and the foresight we now literalize as planning. She gave skills and inventive devices, and wove together irreconcilable factions—weaving of wool was one of those skills and "belonged" to Athene. From Athene's perspective, we might say, the soul of the civilized city was like a fabric, an integrated fabrication laboriously constructed by many minds and many hands.

To keep civic order means keeping youth in line. Athene was patroness of the men's societies called *phratria*[3]—rather like clubs or fraternities or guilds—that wove together young men with civic feeling. As well, she protected the institution of marriage: parents took their daughters to the Athenian acropolis before marriage to bring them under her aegis. Athene's mind, and its civilizing ideals, furthered the progress of an intelligent civic order. Her influence extended to Rome where she became Minerva, one of that city's great triad of ruling dominants. Her complex mind was there given to simpler, practical civilizing skills: Roman roads and arches, Roman laws, schools and teachers, and schools where teachers learn, "normal" schools as we call them. To civilize, Minerva-Athene normalizes.[44]

The term "normal" comes from *norma,* a Latin word meaning a carpenter's square. *Normaliter* means in a straight line, directly; *normalis* means according to the square, and *norma* itself is a technical term for a right angle. The right angle is applicable anywhere, universally identical, like the Roman law of the Empire, like the theorems of plane geometry, like the international style of right-angled architecture of Corbusier and Richard Meier. Thus, civilizing the unwieldy land has come to mean normalizing with the straight lines of the surveyor, with plats, overriding actual terrain and the existing boundaries of local cultures. These archetypal roots in language and myth don't die; even today our common speech uses "straight" and "square" for a normalized person.

Athene did not rule alone—there were twelve Olympians and others beside. In fact, Athene had particular trouble with Dionysos, Poseidon, and the goddess of sensual pleasure and sexual love, Aphrodite. Dionysos, frequently referred to as Lord of Souls, with his dancing crowd of followers, his wine, and his underworld relation to cult mysteries and the natural force of life's vitality, was hardly civilized in Athene's sense. No moderation here, no sober prudence or foresight, no defensive strategy or victory; rather, Dionysos was often a victim. His associated animal, the goat, was not allowed on Athene's grounds.

The conflict with the great god of oceans and rivers, Poseidon, lies in the very foundation of the Athenian city. In the beginning, says the myth, both an olive tree and a spring of saltwater appeared miraculously out of the ground. A slim majority of the people, by one vote only, decided for Athene's gift, the olive so necessary for civilization—olive oil for cooking, for lighting, for healing. Yet barely preferable over the wild sea surge, the unpredictable floodings, and the luring deeps.

5

Poseidon and Athene were also conflicted over the gift of the horse: this animal "belonged" to Poseidon, but the controlling bridle was given by Athene.

Control, discipline, order, marriage, and household are central to the city. While Athene reinforced the home and gave honor to its handwork, Dionysos calls young women to desert their tasks and run to the hills to dance. And, while Athene was always called "virgin," Aphrodite was promiscuity itself. She was shown almost or altogether naked, with doves and roses, open to temptation, while Athene is clad in stiff armor with a giant shield that warns, "Keep your distance." These three archetypal powers seize our eyes and loins with desirable embodiments of beauty, flood our emotions, and call us out of the city altogether in youthful riot. Their excess inspires beyond civility and urbanity.

Their diverging styles do show a common trait: subversion, interruption, surprise. Is this not exactly how culture affects civilization, and how the soul of the street often disorders well-made plans? Let me put the distinction this way: Civilization gets the job done as well and reasonably as possible. Culture is song; the song that breaks out in the midst of the job. Civilization looks back to learn and forward with hope. Culture pops up, sprouts in a petri dish. It infiltrates the city, subversively, through the back alleys of disrepute. Like a disease it finds its own carriers. Whether helped or hindered by civilization, culture is essentially autonomous, unpredictable, and largely unlearned. Culture breaks into civilization and is often assimilated by it. Counterculture, avant-garde, street fashion, pop music, dance, and slang become appropriated by civilization. From slum wall to modern art museum in only a few years.

I am trying to insist upon the uncaused, timeless aspects of culture: that it is marked mainly by surprise. Surprise, which means seized by the sudden, is a category of its own, not merely something new. Surprise offers more than novelty; the renewal it brings is a freshening, enlivening, blessing. To confuse novelty with spontaneity keeps us still within the framework of rational development, as if it were possible to develop a surprise. It seems surprise is genuinely so shocking and disruptive that it has to be tamed by comparisons with the known and old. How ready civilization is to disparage cultural surprises with words like

"That's nothing new!" And how often those who would make culture try so hard to do something "new." But "new" and "old" are terms belonging to progressive civilization; they are curses when applied to culture. The soul is neither new nor old, or it is both at once, utterly fresh as each morning's dream yet rooted in archaic patterns of eternal myths.

Culture does not so much evolve or decline. It seems rather to appear and disappear. For a while in this city, this *quartier,* this cafe, this theater troop or little magazine, architecture team, or graduate department, there is a flourishing. Then it goes elsewhere. Its origins are mysterious and its endings sometimes explosive, or accidental, or simply peter out. In this sense culture has more than linguistic affinities with the occult and the cult. The beginnings of my own field in Vienna and Zurich and its later peculiar blooming in Paris show this combination of cult, occult, and culture. Above all, it is a shared phenomenon in which the little groups involved are themselves surprised by their shared love for their common imagining, becoming soul brothers and soul sisters.

Think of the motley few in Elizabethan taverns who gave English its marvelous language, the few who made the German Romantic movement, think of the intellectuals in Vienna before World War I, of Mistra in the late Middle Ages, Ficino's academy, friends of the heart, in Florence in the fifteenth century that reinspired cultures across Europe, Dada in Zurich, Bloomsbury, Silicon Valley, Black Mountain College, the painters, their critics, their women in Manhattan in the 1950s, the few friends who became the "Invisible College" that began the Royal Society. Think also of four young guys and their girls in a Liverpool garage. Small groups sharing each other's minds, madnesses, and mattresses. The French Revolution began, it is claimed, with a conversation in a Parisian cafe. Did Liverpool, did Providence recreate themselves so surprisingly owing to a common inspiration within a small group? Did the renewal of these two cities arise from Athenian wise counsel alone, or was something else at work?

Perhaps the general term "culture" is too civilized; perhaps there are only subcultures, countercultures, emerging cultures, lost cultures, and culture clashes. Perhaps the city that can pride itself on its culture will boast less of its symphony orchestra and foreign movie theatres, but rather of the mix of differences—backgrounds, social experiments, distinct neighborhoods, historical remnants— and of a general sense of possibility that here in this city something can begin, something generative, non-conforming, unhampered by the city as such, a place where Aphrodite or Dionysos or Poseidon, or any other of the immortals and the Muses, may alight awhile, and smile.

Please understand that my references to myths, my reliance on myths is for the sake of imagination. These myths were the source of the incredible imaginative powers of the Greeks in every field—the sciences, mathematics, architecture, city-building, warfare, political theory, language, and philosophy, as well as the arts, especially theater. The Greek mind so filled with myths continues to nourish imagination, for these myths are a primordial source of both Western culture and Western civilization long ago and still today.

Notes

[1] Ann Shearer, *Athene, Image and Energy* (London/NY: Viking Arkana, 1996), 21–28.
[2] W.B. Stanford, "The Favorite of Athene," in *The Ulysses Theme* (Dallas: Spring Publications, 1992).
[3] Karl Kerenyi, *Athene: Virgin and Mother in Greek Religion* (Dallas: Spring Publications, 1988).
[4] James Hillman, "On the Necessity of Abnormal Psychology: Ananke and Athene," in *Mythical Figures, Uniform Edition of the Writings of James Hillman*, vol. 6.1 (Putnam, CT: Spring Publications, 2007).

THE DANCE OF LEARNING

Thomas Moore

One day my daughter Siobhán was sitting on the bed with my wife and me when I noticed a swelling on her neck. I have had thyroid problems for thirty years, and there was no mistaking that bump. It turned out she had Hashimoto's Disease, an autoimmune disorder that affects the thyroid. She was fourteen and just starting a new life in an excellent local high school. She did well in school, but she couldn't handle the load of homework and the long hours. She would get up at 6 a.m. and still be finishing the day's homework near midnight. She was beginning to look chronically sick and exhausted. So, we decided to homeschool.

I have been interested in education all my adult life. In graduate school I took elective courses in alternative forms of learning and creativity. I received training in Rogerian client-centered psychotherapy, not with the idea of becoming a therapist but to help me as a teacher. I have taught all grades and ages. I've given private music lessons and have spent years giving workshops and seminars in many places. In all this experience I have experimented and used my imagination to seek out every form of learning I could come up with.

I remember giving a child piano lessons. In addition to the usual scales and simple pieces, I had him composing a piece at the keyboard with his elbows and arms and hitting the side of the instrument, using it as a drum. I was trying to have him become less focused on the mechanics of his fingering and more on the basic forms through which sound becomes music. I have taught college courses in which I invited students on the first day of class to choose their grades on the basis of quantity of work involved. I have also used meditation, guided imagery, sleep, and dreams in the classroom.

One of my most enjoyable experiments took place the year I spent teaching humanistic psychology at a state school. I was given a three-hour slot in the schedule to teach older students, using no textbooks and having no curriculum or course design. I just walked into the room once a week and dealt with whatever came up. I did nothing to start the class but only responded, with the idea of teaching something of importance. Recently, in a workshop for psychotherapists in London, I used the same method.

So when my daughter needed an alternative to school, I was interested in being her teacher. She is a bright, lively girl of fifteen who apparently picked up musical talent from me and artistic ability from her mother. She is a quick learner, but she is also a real teenager—she has little patience with things that don't interest her, and she is eager to think up and begin projects but not always to complete them. She's not bookish and can spend enjoyable hours in front of the television watching programs in which her mother and I have no interest. Yet, in homeschooling she has taught me countless lessons about teaching and learning.

At the beginning, we set out a curriculum and a plan that pleased us both. We brought the high school experience into our home—specific times for each subject, a plan for the four years, books and materials and ideas for field work. Within a week or two the entire vision fell apart. She slept in, due in part to her Hashimoto's fatigue, getting up later than the first assigned class. She did amazingly well in certain areas and showed little interest in others. My wife noticed what was going on and asked me nervously whether Siobhán would be ready for college.

I kept thinking: "We're just beginning. We're learning how to do this kind of schooling. Next year we'll get back on track and start over with a firm curriculum." I think they call such idle thoughts whistling in the dark. In fact, I had to rethink what homeschooling was all about and how to teach a teenager.

One of the most helpful and challenging ideas I came up with was to follow my daughter's initiative, rather than force her to squeeze into my ideas about the content and form of learning. I imagine our lessons now as a dance in which I follow and she leads. When a decision has to be made about the schooling, at first I'm tempted to blurt out a solution, but I catch myself and say, "What do you think? What do you want to do?" I find that this way the eros remains in her sphere. Her passion grows and has its own tempo. She accomplishes more and does it happily.

It has taken me a while to adjust to teaching by following rather than by leading. But I'm reminded of Eugene Ionesco's play *The Lesson*,[1] in which a student studies with a teacher with the idea of attaining a total doctorate. The setting is much like homeschooling, with the two of them learning both basic and advanced material. The student is excellent at adding, for example, but can't subtract. But, as a metaphor about life, that's a problem for all of us. Eventually, the teacher becomes so enraged and impassioned that he assaults the student.

In my book on sado-masochism,[2] I explore the power struggles that take place between teacher and student. I see learning in general as a Sadeian enterprise. By that I don't mean the symptomatic and dangerous fall into actual sadism and masochism but rather the need for a degree of constructive power and submission. To avoid sado-masochism I think it's best to allow strength and vulnerability and control and submission to interplay like the intersecting curves of the traditional Taoist symbol, in which black and white areas curve into each other.

So, in our schooling I don't surrender to my daughter; I allow her considerable freedom of choice—but I think it's important to maintain the role of parent with flexible authority. When our desires bump up against each other, I give in to the movement as fully and gracefully as I can. I try to tango with her.

I have discovered that she likes and needs order in certain areas of her learning, areas that often surprise me. When she asks for a list of guidelines for a task or wants a test in a subject, at first I berate myself for not being more organized and having thought of these things myself, and then I realize that I only have to get back into the dance.

We have a friend in her twenties, a young woman Siobhán has known since she was a toddler who comes once a week to tutor her in math. Her tutor gives intense sessions and a lot of homework. I am relieved to see how much those lessons look like school. Siobhán also goes weekly to a class taught by a man in town who teaches teenagers how to build a battery-powered car. There she works with a team of her peers and has responsibility for certain areas of production.

She hangs out with about ten fellow homeschoolers from our small town, so she has an active social life. These boys and girls are all talented in various arts and have a strong desire to learn. Siobhán finds this companionship more supportive of learning than that offered by the young people she knew in her former high school.

As I lecture in many regions and countries as part of my work, I find that people generally lack wit, critical judgment, and a background in reading and ideas. So I help create a curriculum for Siobhán that accentuates these elements. She has read selections from a variety of authors: T.S. Eliot, Samuel Beckett, Ernest Hemingway, Emily Dickinson, Charles Dickens, Ralph Ellison, James Joyce, Robert Frost, Dylan Thomas, Jamaica Kincaid, e.e. cummings, and Mary Oliver. Some of the selections, my favorites in the whole of literature, she brushes off as "boring" or badly written. Others appeal to her. Her favorite so far is James Joyce's short story "Araby," which has influenced her own writing considerably. We have danced jigs in English all year long.

We both wanted to delve into classical Greek culture, but after a bad try at building a model temple, we allowed the Greeks to trail off into oblivion. We got excited about theories on when and how the first inhabitants of America arrived, but then we spent three hours watching a documentary on Benjamin Franklin that only I found fascinating. Siobhán didn't like the near-dead male authorities who served as the requisite talking heads for the program. We hope to do better with Ken Burns' film *Thomas Jefferson*.

Music is perhaps our best subject. I studied music composition and history for seven years in college and tutored students in music theory when I was an undergraduate. This is one field I clearly know and love. Siobhán wants to compose at the piano, and she does it extremely well. But for years I haven't been able to convince her to learn to read music. She reminds me of the great Irish and Scottish musicians I've worked with who couldn't read a note or spell out a chord.

In the car, she hates it when I listen to Bach or some other classical composer. She can't believe I spent my adolescence listening to those boring dead males. But then in homeschooling she rediscovered the flute—she had taken lessons in grade school for a couple of years—and now wants me to accompany her daily on pieces by Vitali, Corelli, Pachelbel, and Saint-Saens. She is facile at parts of the treble clef that I have to guess at.

For English, we study vocabulary, and she has come to love etymologies. We bring a critical eye to newspaper and magazine writing and even to the classics. There are some popular contemporary poets she dismisses for their easy and obvious metaphors and references. She tells me that her own writing has improved a great deal. She reads over the pieces she wrote in her former high school and can't understand how she has learned to write so much better. Apparently she doesn't see the time we spend studying the styles of classic writers as learning how to write. I hope we can continue keeping those lessons under the radar of her attention.

It isn't difficult to see lessons in character and relationship embedded in all of these aspects of learning. Siobhán and I have always been close, but now the companionship is intense. We have deep joy and occasional tension almost every day as together we explore ideas and arts and information.

I watch the dynamics of our interactions closely. Emotions like desire, anxiety, attraction, love, disgust, and longing are the fuel of learning. The content moves or stalls, depending on how you respect these emotions. They are all aspects of eros, of course, and on the principle that psyche follows eros, the only way toward a soul-centered education is to honor desire and all of its positive and negative offshoots. Siobhán and I waltz with desire, allowing the negative, to a point. We don't let negativity spoil the dance or the learning.

I don't know whether child-centered education could work in a school, but I don't see why it wouldn't. The teaching would have to be extraordinarily flexible, allowing for extreme individuality in both student and teacher and capable of moving with the day's emotions. Learning is a kind of movement, a dance, a partnership in which certain kinds of love can keep learning alive.

Discipline has a place, but it is inspired by love and desire, not by edict and tradition. Siobhán and I have set down to our lessons among books and papers in her bedroom, at the breakfast table, and in the kitchen. One day I presented her with a CD set of French lessons. She disappeared for several hours and then returned to tell me she had gone through them all. That's discipline without externally applied pain. One day I gave her a kit for testing water, and she spent the day in the kitchen testing every form of water in sight.

I have always placed musical instruments in the house with the idea that maybe one day someone in the family would take one up and learn it. Once, I bought a reed harmonium made in India and put it in a room. Siobhán came home, saw it, and disappeared. Within a few hours she had figured it out and was chanting Indian tunes while working the bellows with one hand and the keyboard with the other. I have never put any pressure on her learning the instruments but have only made them available. I have put plenty of drums in the house, but they have been more decorative than musical. I have been pushy about learning to read music, and it hasn't fully happened.

For a brief period Siobhán's brother Abe was home from school and studied English with us. I could sense the usual sibling tensions, which occasionally came to the foreground, but overall the arrangement was a real success, in spite of the three-year gap between the two. Tension doesn't have to be an obstacle to learning but can be the sand in the oyster. I think the two learned from each other, even if they didn't want to.

Education is never an objective enterprise; it is always colored by a strong fantasy about it. I enjoy homeschooling because it takes place at home and absorbs many of the values of home. It's intimate, familiar, relaxed, and affected by the tone of home and family. Some homeschoolers refer to their kind of learning as "unschooling." I think it might be good for schools to adopt the fantasy of home. My friend Satish Kumar, founder of the magazine *Resurgence* and of Schumacher College, often tells the story of how he started a school in his village in England by centering it around lunch. He had the children participate in preparing the food and tried to have fresh, good, ethically obtained food for his students. That plan invites fantasies of home and creates community.

The spirit that governs much of modern education is saturnine, after the weighty father god of the Romans and Greeks. A saturnine school would be well-ordered, heavy with authority, aiming at specific goals, full of carefully allocated fields of study and bits of information, and solid and weighty. But it would also be depressive, cool, solitary, formal, traditional, quantitative, and abstract.

My friend John Moriarty, who died in 2007 just as he was making progress toward founding a "hedge school" near where he lived in County Kerry, Ireland, had a different, richer fantasy about education. The hedge schools in Ireland were the people's effort to teach their children behind hedgerows when the English were occupying the country and outlawed education. So there was a subversive fantasy in John's idea—he wanted to form a lay spiritual community, restoring the spirit of early Irish monasticism, which he knew so well, but with the memory of daring resistance to authority.

John's strong feeling for education took him out of the classroom, too. Maybe the very idea of the classroom sometimes gets in the way of learning. Epicurus, it is said, taught in a garden. Marsilio Ficino, an Epicurean and Platonist, taught in a Tuscan villa that had a beautiful loggia and a garden full of mysterious sculpture. Thomas More taught his children at home and went out of his way to fill it with music, interesting visitors, and the classics of literature.

Lao-Tzu wrote: "Without stirring abroad, one can know the whole world; without looking out of the window, one can see the way of heaven. The further one goes the less one knows."[3] A sense of home, intimacy, stillness, adventure without experience, the dance of relationship—these are the ingredients of an education in the soul. Setting goals in education should be a playful setting up for disaster, failure, and disillusionment. The collapse of the goal allows for learning to take place.

Learning what you set out to learn is a contradiction. You learn when you least expect to learn. You learn when you're not trying hard to learn. Nicolas of Cusa, an extraordinarily creative writer of the early fifteenth century, said that learning is like a ball game in which you try to hit a target with a ball, but the ball is hollowed out on one side and wobbles. The point is that learning is a form of play. Nicolas said, in his most popular book, *Educated Ignorance*, that the most important thing to learn is that you don't know what you think you know.

Among educators I sometimes get the feeling that for them learning is a form of defense. It's a way to pretend that you know things that you will never know. This is a particular problem for psychologists, who have a strong need to know about human experience so they can feel competent in helping others. But if their learning is defensive, it will ultimately corrupt their work. Following Cusa, it would be better to know at every point that learning is always a step into ignorance, and that is how it should be.

I find, as a homeschooler, that I have to learn this lesson daily. I'd like to teach my daughter, but she is always undoing my goals and plans and teaching me. I don't go gracefully into my ignorance but learn its intricacies the hard way, day after day. I discover that in the unraveling of my plans and in the discovery of my ignorance, my daughter learns.

Education is a form of play. It's full of illusions, but note that the word "illusion" comes from *in-ludere*, to be in play. We playact the roles of teacher and student, and my daughter is smart enough to see through the seriousness of it all; she is aware of the irony. There is room to move because the educational efforts are play.

In Ionesco's disturbing drama, the teacher and student decide to go for the "total doctorate," nothing less. I think that's what I have in mind in homeschooling my daughter. My fantasy is to have her learn completely. As I mentioned earlier, Ionesco's student is excellent at adding but not at subtracting. That is where we all are: we are good at coming up with more things to learn, while we don't know how to live with our ignorance or give up ideas that we cling to. Lewis Carroll said something similar when he laid out the basics of arithmetic: ambition, distraction, uglification, and derision—the shadows of learning.[4]

I often tell groups I'm teaching that I hope to take some things away from them—a few cherished ideas and assumptions. Otherwise, there will be no learning. I am the Sadeian teacher. I do the subtracting. I have a dark job to do. Educators sometimes cover over the shadow aspect of their work by sentimentalizing teaching or going too far in ennobling it.

Teachers often have the idea that they know things you don't know, and they're going to give you those things. The fact is, they don't know as much as they think they know, and at some level you don't want them giving you anything. Something in you doesn't want to learn, and that resistance is essential to learning, even if it drives your teachers crazy.

This is one way to read the mythic story of Daphne and Apollo. Apollo is the great god of knowledge and healing, and Daphne is a follower of Artemis, the patroness of purity and integrity. In the story of Ovid, Daphne runs away from Apollo, who is attracted to her and wants to befriend her. She wants nothing to do with his intellect and skills. As he runs, he tells her how great he is and how much he knows. In response, she begs her father for help, and he turns her into a tree.

Students are often in the Daphne position: something trustworthy in them resists being acculturated. They don't want to lose their naturalness and individuality. They would rather have a wooden mind than succumb to the well-intentioned teachings of the one pursuing them.

When women hear the story of Daphne today, they often read it as a sexual assault, and indeed there is a strong Sadeian tone to the story. The enlightened teacher, only wanting the best for his, or even her, students, embodies the dark side of Apollo, the chaser and potential attacker. Although Apollo is not just a male—he is the archetype of reason and enlightenment—he is a threat, and any teacher should know that his wonderful wishes for his students may look monstrous to them, at least in a subliminal way. The dance becomes a tarantella, a dance rooted in the sting of a tarantula.

The only solution to the Daphne myth in education is to take it on. Appreciate what Daphne needs. Appreciate what you need as a teacher. Do both: teach and hold back. Go forward and backward, as in a dance. Sidestep. Move your shoulders. Sway your hips.

My daughter, like many teenage girls, is spilling over with Daphne spirit. She is warm and close, and yet something in her doesn't want to be compromised. If I don't identify too much with Apollo but only let his spirit have some influence, she will learn something. But she will be herself. She may never read piano music, as much as I wish she would. She may not study the sciences, as I hope she will. Heaven forbid, she may go in her own direction.

Aristotle says that the soul grants a thing its identity. It makes an axe an axe, he says. I hope that a soul-motivated education will make my daughter who she is, not what I want her to be.

Contemporary education is led in large part by anxiety: worry about children making it in the world, having a profession or trade, keeping up with competing nations, staying abreast of changes in knowledge and culture, and making enough money. What if we were to shed those anxieties and think positively about education, about helping our children become who they were born to be and to make a unique contribution to society? Maybe then teaching and learning would move to the music of the Muses and the choreography of the Graces.

Notes

[1] Eugene Ionesco, *Four Plays: The Bald Soprano; The Lesson; Jack, or the Submission; The Chairs* (Brooklyn, NY: Grove Press, 1994).
[2] Thomas Moore, *Dark Eros: The Imagination of Sadism* (Putnam, CT: Spring Publications, 1995).

[3] Lao Tzu. *Tao Te Ching,* trans. D.C. Lau (New York: Penguin Classics, 1963), xl.
[4] Lewis Carol, *Alice in Wonderland and Through the Looking Glass* (New York: Signet Classics, 2000).

CHRONOS VERSUS KAIROS: A PLEA FOR THE RESTORATION OF EMPATHY AND IMAGINATION IN HISTORY TEACHING

Ruth Meyer

The year is 1997. I am teaching history in a high school on the outer fringes of London, England. My native Great Britain is at the height of its testing frenzy induced by Prime Minister Tony Blair's promise to raise standards with a "National Curriculum in Education," a project inherited from the previous government under Margaret Thatcher and her successor, John Major. An ominous new militaristic vocabulary is entering my history teacher's world. Task forces are sent by the government to reform failing schools. Teachers are told they must meet new government-set targets. Just like the troops on a battlefield, historical facts must now be selected and deployed with precision to meet the targets. An atmosphere of anxiety pervades the teachers' lounge. In the mornings we mutter complaints over our tea and gather in groups whispering in hushed tones. By morning recess over more tea and fired up by sugary cookies, we mutter in louder tones, but since no one has come up with a plan to counterattack, we sigh and pencil in extra meetings after school hours to meet the government's expectations.

I have a dream. I am in the middle of a Nazi concentration camp. A bouquet of barbed wire surrounds me in a black metallic circle, like a wreath. The words *Arbeit Macht Frei* (Work Makes you Free) appear above this circle, just as they appear in reality above the entrance to

Auschwitz. I recognize this as a big dream. I am terrified and mystified. My whole body feels trapped in this camp, yet there appears to be a small hope of freedom. I ponder the dream. In my working world I am in the midst of teaching Nazi Germany and the Holocaust to my students. Are we all trapped in the testing camp? Are the new tests part of the concentration camp? What is the work that I must do to set us free?

Although I don't yet know it, this dream has a large trajectory. In two years time I will be leaving London and exchanging my history classroom in England for one in San Jose, California. In an effort to gain a new perspective on history and education, to break free from the concentration camp, I will sell my house in London and enroll in a Ph.D. program in Depth Psychology at Pacifica Graduate Institute near Santa Barbara, California.

At the time of this dream, I am twelve years into my teaching career, and disheartened. My favorite teaching objective, historical empathy, is being abandoned because critics say it is too imprecise—it can't be measured. Mrs. Thatcher, Britain's former Prime Minister and architect of a new National Curriculum for Britain's schools has asserted:

History is an account of what happened in the past. Learning history, therefore, requires knowledge of events. It is impossible to make sense of such events without absorbing sufficient factual information and without being able to place matters in a clear chronological framework—which means knowing dates. No amount of imaginative sympathy for historical characters or situations can be a substitute for the initially tedious but ultimately rewarding business of memorizing what actually happened.[1]

Yet "imaginative sympathy" was the part of history teaching that my students enjoyed the most. Historical empathy was the buzz word in history teaching for entering into another world. It was all the rage amongst British history teachers in the 1980s. Historical empathy is the gift shared by so many wonderful historians, such as Simon Schama and Fernand Braudel; it rests on the ability to take oneself back into another time and place. It is the capacity to enter into another's shoes—to imagine walking with the Romans as they marched into Gaul, to march with the Normans into new territory at Hastings,

England, or to protest with the French women as they traversed the eighteen kilometers from Paris to Versailles in 1789 demanding bread. The concept was popular when I first trained as a history teacher at Oxford University's Department of Educational Studies in 1985. But in the educational reforms of the 1990s, it was dropped.

Back in the 1980s we would form family units in my history class and attempt to enter the world of inflation and political extremism in Weimar, Germany in 1928. My students would set tables ready for dinner, only to find that there was very little to eat. I would assign students family roles, and I would flit from table to table eavesdropping, as father returned from work to find two tearful children at his dinner table asking why they only had turnip soup (yet again). Sometimes an older sibling would come to the dinner table full of enthusiasm after attending a Communist Party rally, and a heated political discussion would ensue. Could he persuade his parents to join him at the next rally? Or were they conservatives, fearing change and worrying about traditional values?

Around the time that historical empathy was assassinated, I saw a cartoon in *The Times Educational Supplement* (Britain's paper for teachers). A student sat at his desk in his home, head in his hands, with piles of textbooks and study guides spilling over into unruly piles on the floor. The implication was that he was preparing for his new Key Stage 3 National Curriculum tests (the closest United States equivalent would be SATs, although Key Stage 3 tests are taken at age 13–14, or at the end of 8th grade). At his side were some discarded toys and a jar in a garbage can labeled "childhood."

As I became more and more depressed about this state of affairs, I felt as if I were indeed part of the huge concentration camp in my dream. Each day at school, as more and more government inspections and educational targets came my way, I felt as if all of us teachers and students alike were trapped in this new hothouse of concentration and forced learning. Each day became a grind. The joy was vanishing. I decided to leave England and study at Pacifica. At my interview I told Dr. Dianne Skafte that I wanted to research the value of historical empathy and to do something about reforming education. My acceptance at Pacifica gave me the benefit of distancing myself from education in England and focusing instead on the value of historical imagination, as seen through the lens of depth psychology.

As I studied the problem of testing and learned more about

mythology, I realized that British educators, and it seems their American counterparts, have become obsessed with measurement. "A topic isn't worth teaching unless it can be measured," I was told at one teacher's conference in London. The effect of this obsession is that history teaching now is dominated by the values of the God Chronos. This particular Greek God is not a very likeable fellow, especially if viewed through the Spanish artist Goya's eyes as a crazed, wild-eyed god gnawing on his child's torso. Is our system of testing eating up our children, consuming their childhoods, depriving them of sleep, force-feeding them on a diet of dry-bone facts, dates, and timelines to be memorized and measured?

Chronos time is characterized by the nervous clock-watching that teachers observe when proctoring tests. Like sprinters the students take on the God of Time as they race for the finish line, trying to outpace him by ever-faster thinking and writing. Chronos history is dominated by the testing calendar, linear thinking and document-based questions that are taught according to formulas. Biographies of important characters in world history are included only if they contain some *useful* information that might shed insight on the current educational targets, or standards, as they are called here in California. Thus in my current A.P. World History textbook the amazing early years of Alexander the Great are reduced to a paragraph, entirely omitting any of the delicious morsels of information that might shed light on his personality and the times in which he lived. Instead, his dates are given. There is a sentence to say that his tutor was Aristotle, but missing are the stories we find in Arrian and Plutarch of his mother's prophetic dream on her wedding night, the taming of the horse Bucepahalus who was afraid of his shadow, and Alexander's belief in omens, oracles, and destiny. Even the wonderful story of the Gordian knot has been cut out.

In *The Soul's Code*, James Hillman believes we have been robbed of our true biographies such that we turn to therapy in later life to rediscover them.[2] I would like to take this thought a stage further and consider the notion that at school we have been robbed of our true histories, so we turn in later life to memoir writing, genealogy tracing, and life story workshops to rediscover what was missing from our education. Soul history cannot be destroyed. It may be driven underground, but it will reemerge sooner or later in a myriad of ways. Perhaps through coin collecting or reenacting battles from the Civil

War. Perhaps through collecting old photographs, volunteering at a local museum, or developing an interest in Native American quilting patterns.[3] History will reemerge because it is a basic human need to feel a sense of community, rootedness, and belonging. Our ancestors' voices are out there, waiting to be heard.

Hillman's *The Soul's Code* is a radical departure from the realm of Chronos. The dreams, accidents, visionary moments, quirks of fate, and synchronicities that make up the biographies in *The Soul's Code* are part of a different dimension of time. The Greeks called this Kairos time. There is an altogether different quality about it. Whereas Chronos is heavy and burdened, constricted by the clock and limited time, Kairos time can be playful, elastic, and unbounded. A Kairos moment is a soul moment, a moment in which time takes on a deeper dimension of vertical rather than horizontal proportions. It could be a moment of inspiration.

I think of Clio, the Greek muse of history, and her sisters dancing in a circle around the springs on Mount Olympus and Mount Helicon. She steps lightly, the Greek poet Hesiod tells us.[4] Her role is to inspire the poet and so to breathe new life into history. As I studied the stories of Clio and her sisters, I realized that the circle of muses represents an antidote to the constraining circle of barbed wire in the concentration camp dream. The circle of barbed wire imprisons and constrains. The circle of muses contains and liberates. A muse visitation puts the writer in a state of flow. Just as the circular dances of the muses flow naturally like spring waters, so imaginative writing can flow freely when the writer is in this inspired state of mind. When I look at artistic representations of Clio and her sisters, I am reminded of children dancing in a circle, inviting others to join them in their fun.

The publication of *The Soul's Code* in 1997 was very timely for me.[5] I read it when I was right in the midst of my depression provoked by the turn in British education. The crux of the matter, as the dream suggested, centered on my teaching of the Holocaust. Because Britain suffered so much during the Second World War, many history courses focus on Nazi Germany and the Holocaust. I was horrified at the testing questions on this topic being set by my examination board in London. Students were given tables of statistics of deaths of Jews in Poland, Germany, Hungary, Rumania, the USSR, the Netherlands, Lithuania, France, Austria, and Czechoslovakia; a short extract from the minutes of the Wannsee conference in 1942 when Hitler's henchmen decided upon their "final solution;" and a ghastly black-and-white photo of the ovens at Auschwitz. Students were then expected to "select and deploy" their factual knowledge to answer questions based on these extracts.

Where were the stories of families whose lives were affected by these events? Where were their names? To reduce the teaching of the Holocaust to tables of statistics and Nazi euphemisms for murder is to reinforce the dehumanizing process that the Nazis had originally created. It seemed to me that in the race to improve standards in education, the British government was repeating some of the traumas of the Second World War and inflicting them on the young.

Just before I left England for the United States, I attended a workshop for Holocaust educators run by an organization called *Facing History and Ourselves* (FHAO). I saw the flyer advertising the course in London's Weiner Library (a small library dedicated to the study of Jewish history). I had been visiting the library regularly in the hope of creating alternative assessments for my students as an antidote to the type of examination questions described above. I had been immersing myself in Holocaust survivor's stories in an effort to put human faces on these dehumanizing events. As I walked down the library's stairs one day, a flyer pinned to the library's notice board caught my eye. It was my call to adventure. I remember a warm rush of energy entering my heart as I read about it. A magnetic pull of intuition entered my body. A veil seemed to lift momentarily to offer me a fleeting glimpse of new possibilities. An aperture appeared in the fence of that concentration camp in my dream, and I seized the opportunity to make a run for educational freedom.

I loved the very name: *Facing History and Ourselves*. It seemed to suggest that history is a reflective activity where we are faced with reflections of our own lives and then invited to enter into community to join our lives with the lives of our ancestors. As soon as I saw the flyer announcing that the group was holding an international workshop for Holocaust educators, I wanted to go. The title carries within it the image of the mirror of history. All too often, students are asked to gaze into history without ever seeing their own reflection. *Facing History* tries to end this one-sided approach. Their in-depth manner of teaching the Holocaust constantly requires students to ask themselves: how would you have acted in this situation? Often, it's not facing history that is the difficult task but, rather, facing ourselves.

Facing History and Ourselves is a nonprofit organization based in Brookline, Massachusetts. The program has been working for nearly two decades to combat racism and prejudice through an in-depth study of the hard history of the Holocaust. Although they do not explicitly say so, the FHAO approach incorporates the Jungian concept of shadow. Jung describes the shadow as the "dark aspects of the personality" which are pushed into the unconscious.[6] These are the rejected parts of ourselves that we would rather not know about. In the process known as projection, we push these disowned parts onto others. As FHAO states in 1994:

With the guidance of support of the Facing History staff and resource speakers, teachers and students explore the roots of religious, racial, and ethnic hatreds, and their consequences. And they come to realize that "the shadowy figures that look at us from the tarnished mirror of history" are—in the final analysis— ourselves.[7]

In this statement of intent, we see that we are required not just to look for reflections of ourselves in the history—but to face up to reflections of our own shadow that we may want to deny.

FHAO rented an old oak-paneled stately home in Oxfordshire, complete with suits of armor and coats of arms. Here in this dignified setting, replete with its own fascinating history, educators from all over the world converged for a five-day residential retreat. Each day I attended workshops with Holocaust survivors. There was Rudi, now in his seventies but still standing tall and full of aristocratic poise. It was hard to believe that this six-foot Dutchman had once been confined to the cramped living quarters of a secret section of a house, where he was sheltered during the war like Anne Frank. Present too was Greta, a graceful Auschwitz survivor from Hungary who was now living in Sweden and working on her memoirs. These survivors restored the human dimension of the Holocaust that had been missing in my government-sponsored history assignments. Listening to their testimonies and learning how to teach the Holocaust in such a way as to invite reflection and participation from the students filled me with hope. When the course was over, I drove fifty miles north to my family home in Coventry and spent a week with my mother, herself an evacuee from the 1940 German bombing raids on the city. As I lay on my bed in my hometown, I experienced a type of waking dream. It was still light outside, and I had gone to bed early to read. I had not yet fallen asleep. A gentle whispering, rushing sound seemed to fill the air around me. "Teach," the Holocaust survivors were whispering to me. "Go out and teach about us. Teach soul history, and teach so that no one will ever forget us."

Three years later, I found myself in California repeating this experience. Summer fieldwork is an important element of the Ph.D. program in Depth Psychology at Pacifica Graduate Institute. At the end of my first year of studies I was called once again to attend a *Facing History* workshop and to listen into the heart and soul of the world speaking through its participants. In June 2000 I attended a *Facing History* Summer Institute for Holocaust educators held in a convent in the Santa Cruz Mountains. Our leader was Jack Weinstein of the Bay Area branch of FHAO. Once more, the beautiful accommodations and peaceful surroundings seemed to evoke reflection and insight amongst the participants. Once more, survivors came to share their stories with us. Kairos time opened up for me again as I listened to Gloria tell her story of how she escaped from a concentration camp to freedom. For a few moments I was with her crouching in fear, hiding from the Nazi guards. I shivered, even through the heat of a July afternoon in California with temperatures in the high eighties, because I was back with Gloria, crouching with her through the severity of the winter in Eastern Europe.

When a survivor tells her story, Chronos takes a back seat. Linear time recedes, and the listener becomes enthralled by the story, journeying back with the survivor to the 1940s. Speaking from memory and from the heart, survivors can take a listener back in time so that one is right there beside them, living and breathing their experience. That night my fellow teachers reported amazing dreams of teaching history in new empowering ways. Sleeping in the whitewashed simple bedrooms of the convent helped create sacred space for new dreams to break through. I dreamed I was back in London, England, teaching in Hampstead, the final home of Nazi refugee Sigmund Freud and the current home to many of England's finest dream workers, including the Tavistock clinic. The golden leaves of autumn fell in the square as I perched at a podium on a raised platform with one of my former history students, sharing my newfound knowledge of Holocaust history teaching with the audience.

The most memorable teaching aid I take from my five days in the Santa Cruz Mountains is the Soul History Chart. *Facing History* calls this an identity map, but I prefer "Soul History Chart" because the exercise embodies some of Hillman's teaching in the *The Soul's Code*. FHAO has developed a lesson using identity maps to help us begin to reflect on some of those more soulful moments that help to shape our history. When I attended my second Summer Institute with FHAO in California's Bay Area in June 2000, I learned how to make my own identity map. Part of the beauty of this exercise is that it is so simple. All one needs is a large piece of paper, a marker, and several different colored packs of Post-Its. Usually when we are asked to define our identity, we use categories such as gender, age, height, hair color, weight, and also ties to a particular religion, class, neighborhood, school, or nation. This exercise invites us to delve a little deeper. The aim is to reach beyond persona and into soul.

The first task is to draw an outline of a shape for the identity map. I chose to draw an island, which I called "La Isla Historica"—but others in the group chose circles, crosses, and even people for their outline shapes. Next, using the color-coded Post-Its, we consider special music, special teachers, special places, special films, accidents, vacations, relationships, birthdays, deaths, moments of religious and spiritual significance, and sudden moments of insight. Each color of Post-It is assigned to a particular category: for example, special music could be blue, significant teachers might be pink, etc. Each Post-It should be big enough to write the title of the music or teacher on it. Then, finally, the Post-Its are arranged on the outline shape in whatever pattern is meaningful for each person.

The beauty of this method of working is that it breaks out of the linear model of looking at a life. Furthermore, it honors those special soulful Kairos moments, which are often overlooked when one tells her life story. It helps participants to begin to look at their life story in a totally different way.

My island had a "sea of depression," representing the life events that plunged me into searching for a new path of Holocaust study and ultimately led me to California and my Ph.D. program. Clumped together by the sea were many different color Post-Its: a blue Post-It signifying the sad ending of a love affair, and many green Post-Its for books like *The Bell Jar* by Sylvia Plath, *Memories, Dreams, Reflections* by C. G. Jung, and *Into That Darkness* (an interview with Franz Stangl, the

Nazi commander of Treblinka concentration camp) by Gitta Sereny. These represented life-changing books; there could be movies here too. On the sunnier side of the island were blue Post-Its for new relationships and yellow ones for new places: Yosemite where I was married, Hawaii where I spent my honeymoon, and Pacifica, where I learned the value of imagination, dreams, visions, and trance states in the creative processes of historians.

As James Hillman indicates, it is often "the supposedly trivial moment" that is significant.[8] We were encouraged to consider moments of awakening to new ideas and to add these to our charts. On my identity chart I placed a marker for the moment when I first saw the flyer for the *Facing History* workshop in the Wiener library. Another marker indicated the strange déjà vu moment experienced when I was walking in the gardens of Versailles and suddenly felt an overwhelming sense of grief and despondency. It was as if time had opened up, and I was back in the past, walking with Queen Marie Antoinette and experiencing a sense of foreboding.[9] These are two of my Kairos moments.

Accidents and disappointments figured largely on my map and the maps of others. "Father's alcoholism," "marriage repair," "first love, now over," "car accident in 5th grade," "failing an examination," "breaking my leg skiing"— these are some of the soulful moments that appeared on my colleagues' maps. If the twists of love and the accidents of fate are evidence of soul history, then these maps were living testimony to those ideas.

The identity map exercise is placed right at the beginning of *Facing History's* curriculum. Asking students to consider their special soul moments is a beautiful way to begin the school year. It promotes sharing of meaningful experiences as well as invites reflection and glimpses into the lives of others. It helps create a sense of community in the classroom.

Later in the school year, when students have studied a variety of different characters from world history, I carry out a follow-up of this exercise. I ask them to choose a character from world history to which they feel drawn and to investigate his or her biography in greater detail. Then I ask them to make an identity map for this character in the same way that they constructed their own. Finally, I ask them to discuss the similarities and differences between the two identity maps.

The virtue of this exercise is that it promotes the empathetic connection between the personal story and history. It invites students to observe connections between their lives and the lives of their ancestors, and nurtures the imagination. It allows a group of students to observe how each is called as a unique witness to history through the specificity of his or her own life story.

I seek to engage my students in some type of soul history every week. I am currently engaged in devising a series of writing prompts designed to promote historical empathy. I sneak in imaginative readings such as Enkidu's dream of the underworld from the *Epic of Gilgamesh* or Plutarch's description of Alexander the Great's call to adventure, whenever possible. Through these lessons I aim to escape from the concentration camp atmosphere that pervades so many schools in both the United Kingdom and the United States.

Yet I realize that the effort to open space for Kairos moments to enter the classroom is sometimes too great and these moments are altogether too few. In our current world, Chronos is king. New teachers entering the system in Great Britain will have no notion of those special Kairos moments engendered by historical empathy, and the organization *Facing History and Ourselves* remains a largely American-based phenomenon. However, the degree of depth and reflection required by a *Facing History* course is often all-too-difficult to fit into an American school's Chronos-packed schedule as well. In my own high school we offer the course as a one-semester elective for juniors and seniors. But we sacrifice to Chronos at our peril. Hillman warns us that if we continue to feed our students a diet of "facts rather than thinking, and patriotic, politically or religiously correct 'values' rather than critical judgment [we] may produce a nation of achieving high school graduates who are also psychopaths."[10] For the psychopathic brain can recite formulas and facts to support its world view, but the capacity for empathy for the suffering psychopaths inflict on others will be absent. Also absent will be any degree of engagement or depth.

So I visualize the nine muses dancing in a circle on Mount Olympus whenever I feel under pressure to conform to some new Chronos-based demand. This healing image replaces the barbed-wire wreath of the concentration camp. I am now in my twenty-second year of history teaching. I find that the older I become, the more passionate I feel about the sacred nature of those Kairos moments and the more determined I become to defend the right of every student to an experience of history based on empathy and imagination.

Notes

[1]Margaret Thatcher, *The Downing Street Years 1979-1990* (New York: HarperCollins, 1993), 595.

[2] James Hillman, *The Soul's Code* (New York: Warner Books, 1996),. 5.

[3] Roy Rosenzweig and David P. Thelen, *The Presence of the Past Popular Uses of History in American Life* (New York: Columbia University Press, 1998),. 31–36. These two history professors discuss the failure of America's schools to engage history students, and the amazing reemergence of history in various places in later life.

[4] Hesiod, *Theogony & Works and Days*, trans. M. L. West, World's Classics (Oxford [Oxfordshire]: Oxford University Press, 1988, 5.

[5] Hillman, *The Soul's Code*.

[6] C. G. Jung (1976). "Aion: Phenomenology of the Self" in *The Portable Jung*, ed. J. Campbell (New York: Penguin, 1976), 145.

[7] Facing History and Ourselves, *Resource Book* (Brookline, MA: Facing History and Ourselves National Foundation Inc., 1994), xvii.

[8] Hillman, *The Soul's Code*,. 203.

[9] Marie-Louise von Franz, *Psyche and Matter* (Boston, MA: Shambhala Publications, 1992),. 115. Here von Franz discusses the strange phenomenon of time travel and cites the experiences of two English ladies on the grounds of Versailles. Their experiences mirror my own. She also discusses within this context C.G. Jung's experience in the breakdown of linear time at Ravenna

[10] Hillman, *The Soul's Code*, 5.

GOOD TEACHING DOESN'T COUNT!

David L. Miller

I. What Counts? The Language of Accountability and Assessment

Huston Smith, the renowned philosopher of religions, was for a time a colleague of mine in the Department of Religion at Syracuse University. Huston had taught at MIT in the humanities program before coming to the Department of Religion at Syracuse in 1973. One day he told me about having had lunch with a high-energy particle physicist at MIT. During the course of the lunch the philosopher of religions and the post-quantum mechanics scientist discovered that they had many perspectives in common on matters of cosmos, society, and self. This did not much surprise Huston, but it did surprise the physicist. What surprised Huston was the physicist's way of acknowledging his surprise. The scientist said: "Why, there is only one difference between us. You don't count!"

This pun reveals a great deal. It says that counting, i.e., quantifying things, is for some what counts, i.e., what is of value. Objective outcomes assessment confirms value.

It is often the case that a play in language can provide unexpected discovery. There are leaps in learning hiding in words' metonymies, in the very words people have used to name what they think they are naming when they name things. As Martin Heidegger writes: "It is not we who play with words, but the nature of language plays with us."[1] Wittgenstein says it this way: "A picture [*ein Bild*] held us captive. It lay in our language, and our language repeated it to us inexorably."[2] So, I propose for a moment to look at the two terms in the rhetoric of values

31

assessment in contemporary education. And I begin with the word "accountability."

"Accountability." It goes without saying that both the noun and verb forms of the word "account" come from the noun and verb forms of the word "count," which means "enumeration" or "to compute." The family includes the words "counter" (token) and "countless," as well as the words "putative," "amputate," "compute," "deputation," "dispute," "disputant," "impute," "imputation," "repute" and "reputation." Already the words "amputate" and "dispute" in the lexical complex imply there is some "fight" and some disputed signification in the word before we even use it.

The base for the family is Latin *putare*, meaning (a) ""to prune," (b) ""to purify," "to correct" (an account), therefore also "to count" or "calculate." But whichever sense of *putare*—prune or purify—that our notion of "accounting" comes from, there is implied some pruning (downsizing?) and some implicit political correctness or puritanical self-confidence. In the Sanskrit background, there is a relation to the family of words from which we get the word "pave," Latin *paure*, meaning "to beat" or "tread earth down to level it," i.e., to flatten (mediocrity, democratization). There is also a connection to the Latin *puteus*, meaning "a hole cut in the ground," especially "a well," from which Middle English has the word "pit," meaning a "cavity."

The compounds of *putare* that are relevant to English are *amputare*, "to prune or cut around" (*am-* for *ambi-*, meaning "on both sides"), so "amputation"; *computare*, "to count" (intensive use of *con-*), hence "compute" means "really to count"; *deputare*, "to cut downwards," so to esteem, allot, depute, as in a deputy or deputation; *disputare*, "to think about contentiously"; *imputare*, "to put into the reckoning"; *reputare*, "to reckon or examine accounts again and again, to think over, to credit, so to repute and reputation." There also belong to this family "recount," to count again, or to relate, by way of French *reconter*, since Old French *conter* became differentiated into French *conter*, to tell, and French *compter*, to count.[3]

Think of this verbal complex in relation to the words of the poet: "How do I love thee? Let me count the ways." The poem actually means: *Don't* count! Write a poem! And don't count on *it!* It's the love that counts, not the counting. The jazz standard says: "Will I be in that number when the saints go marchin' in?" But in the singing there is implied the advice: *Don't* count! The number of those saved in the

32

apocalypse (144,000) is not a number, not a numbering. It means to discourage adding things up, like merits. Luther mounted a reformation against that. It you start counting, you might miss the rapture!

"Assessment." There are similar problems with the language of assessment. If one were to bring the perspectives from the business and commercial world, the world of "total quality management" to bear upon assessment in the university, then one might first observe that it is not very high quality management to use the word "assessment" when what one really means is "evaluation." The term "assessment" has become empty jargon, meaning nothing, a real miracle term.

The word has in linguistic tradition actually referred to courts (a judge assesses a fine) and taxation (as in the assessment of property). In the former case, guilt is assumed, and it is just a question of how much one is going to have to pay. In the other case, it is assumed that one should pay, and it is just a question of how much. I well realize that this term has passed from business and commerce, from law and government, into the vernacular and that it merely means "evaluation." I realize, too, that to say "evaluate" education and teaching is not a rhetoric that is inflated enough to make university administrations, boards of education, trustees, and congresspersons sound like they are doing something out of the ordinary. But does the field of education want to ignore precision of ideas and language? Do we really want to use a term that carries these negative, if unconscious, connotations about behavior? Are we accountable about accountability? Are we willing to assess assessment?

There are some philosophers and theorists who have argued that language speaks, not the people who use language. These thinkers have argued that, even if we wanted to, we couldn't be Alice's Humpty Dumpty, who said that words would mean whatever he intended them to mean. Confucius—during a moment of cultural confusion in ancient China—called for a "rectification of names" in the land, for a proper use of language, without which, he seemed to believe, there could be no justice, or truth, or beauty.

The point about language is linked to the story of Huston Smith, who didn't count, according to the pun of his MIT colleague. Smith has argued passionately in his later life and writings for the important value of being accountable to matters that are precisely un-countable.

According to Smith, the unassessables—at least in quantifiable and empirical terms—are the following: (1) qualities, (2) invisibles, (3) meanings that are existential as opposed to cognitive, (4) purposes that are metaphysical as opposed to teleonomical, and (5) values that are normative rather than descriptive. In my view, the experiences that some teaching professionals cherish for students have precisely to do with quality, invisibility, existential meaning, metaphysical purposes, and normative values. For these teachers—in Smith's view—education and teaching are in principle not assessable.

Confucius said: "Do not wish for quick results, nor look for small advantages. If you seek quick results, you will not attain the ultimate goal. If you are led astray by small advantages, you will never accomplish great things."[4] There are no quick results in education. If an educator seeks a quick result, the ultimate goal of great teaching is not accomplished. No assessment is worthwhile until many years have passed. And then the need for assessment has passed anyway.

Besides, any teacher worth her or his salt makes assessments and takes account of the teaching long before making course evaluations or assessing results. Assessing goes on during teaching—mid-course, mid-class, and even often mid-sentence. I call these *mid-course corrections*, a phrase so crucial to aviation, without which activity the flight would not work. Defining goals or learning outcomes in advance is an unnatural way of defending against natural mid-course corrections. It is a defense against the sensitivity that makes great teaching what it is, always and already.

The great teachers—Socrates, Moses, Jesus, Buddha, Confucius, Lao Tzu, Maimonides, al-Ghazzali, for instance—confounded expected outcomes and in principle and iconoclastically made assessment impossible. They would have failed in current attempts to focus on values in education. Their expected outcome was to make impossible the achievement of outcomes that were expected before the teaching began. One desirable learning outcome is not to have a desired learning outcome. Concerning this, let me offer a few aphorisms.

II. Aphorisms

* There is too much talk about teaching these days. It all leads to self-consciousness. No one knows what teaching is. It always must be thought in terms of something else. Metaphor and metonymy are

needed. Imagination and vision. Not counting and assessment.

* Teaching is like baseball. Even in the majors it's not baseball very often. Most of the time it's pretty boring. But sometimes it really is baseball. And then it is really something! While waiting for it to be baseball, what does one do? One plays second base as best one can. Outcomes assessment implies that the value in baseball is that it be baseball all the time. It also implies that the players can control it. But that's not the way things are. Even for the pros. People who call for outcomes assessment don't understand the game. They don't understand the nature of the game.

* There are two things that one learns from baseball: (1) You don't have to swing at every pitch. (2) You know when a pitcher (professor) is tiring when the ball starts rising. It takes a lot of energy and concentration to keep it down. Letting it soar is easy. (I am grateful to James Hillman for this and the earlier baseball metaphor)

* What is impossible is to undertake an evaluation of value in higher education if one takes one's eye off the subject matter and puts it instead on the performance of the teacher and/or the student. Education is not the passing of information from one person who has it to someone who does not. It is not the trading of databases. Rather, the subject matter is a vessel into which the professor and the student place themselves together. And then they see what happens. They observe and take note. It is like alchemy. One cares for the process in the alchemical vessel. It is like two people not loving but being *in* love.

* To speak of "improvement" in teaching is nonsense if the eye is really on the egos of the professor and the student rather than on the subject matter. Do we "improve" the subject matter by our activity? The irony is that attention to desired learning outcomes and to outcomes assessment produces in fact just what it sets out to eradicate: namely, emphasis on the professoriate rather than on the student. Assessment is a narcissistic endeavor. It is not student-centered. It puts the focus of consciousness on questions like "How am *I* doing?" and "How can *I* improve?" We are only student-centered when we have enough regard for the student to focus on the subject matter and to trust students to take care of themselves. They are not stupid. And they are

not children.

* In education, as in sex, sometimes the only way to improve the quality and value of education is to stop focusing on oneself and to stop asking, "Am I doing it well?" Such ego-consciousness can ruin learning just as it can be a pain in the neck to the beloved. When the child says, "Look, Ma, I'm dancing!" she or he is no longer dancing. It is the same with teaching and learning, not to mention loving. If you ask about it, you are not doing it.

* Teaching in the humanities is like the fire-consumed stick in Buddhism. A disciple once asked the Buddha how one should approach his teachings, given that the overall aim of the Buddha's teaching was nonattachment, including nonattachment to the teachings! The Buddha replied that his teaching was like a stick that keeps the fire going, stirring the coals, until the stick is itself consumed by the fire. The stick disappears. There is nothing in the end to assess if the teaching is really successful.

* Think of the parable of the sower in the Gospel of Mark (Mark 4.3–9). It is the various soils that get in the way of the sowing. Or the birds. Not the sower. Imagine assessing the outcome of sowing by evaluating the sower!

* Teaching is improvisation, like good jazz. Does one ask a jazz musician for objectives, goals, outcomes, and ways to achieve outcomes assessment? Good scat is not playing it, but playing with it. In scat, as in *glossolalia*, the discourse is nonmimetic. Good teaching is scat. It is like speaking in tongues. The tongues of the material.

* Being interesting and enthusiastic are not necessarily marks of a good course or teacher. They may well be marks of educational fraud. A famous rabbi, commenting angrily on reports of his renown for preaching, said: "God forbid that I should ever 'talk well.'"[5] This is tantamount to saying: "God forbid that I should ever be a good teacher in terms of conventional criteria of assessment. Then I would not have taught at all."

* There is a sign hanging on a bulletin board down the hall from my

office. It announces "Teaching Tools for the Nineties!" and it promises that if you get these tools your outcomes assessment will be more successful. This sign of our academic times puts me in mind of a line from the 1960 Phi Beta Kappa oration at Columbia University by Norman O Brown. Brown was recapitulating the values expressed in Emerson's Phi Beta Kappa lecture entitled "The American Scholar." In the light of those values, Brown announced, "Fools with tools are still fools."[6]

* Continual assessment and a demand for accountability are symptoms of a sickness, symptoms of the very sickness that they are meant to cure: namely, they are signs that the intrinsic value of education is not sensed or affirmed, that it must be proved. Even when pedagogy fails—as it did again and again with Socrates, Moses, Jesus, Jeremiah, Mohammed, Lao-Tzu, and the Buddha—the attempt to assess learning outcomes is likely the worst possible indicator of accountability, at least in the case of certain pedagogies in certain subject matters. Socrates got hemlock in the assessment; Jesus, the cross; Moses, no promised lands; and there were others! It is even arguable that a negative assessment may indicate that important learning is taking place. It is like the putative course evaluation by a professor at Columbia. One of the questions he asks his students at the end is the following: "Tell which text you liked the least, and explain what character flaw in yourself accounts for this dislike!"

* The political correctness of the eighties has become the pedagogical correctness of the New Age.

* Thomas Green—a renowned philosopher of education—once told me that he thought the only useful question to ask students in course evaluation was the following: "What will you now not put up with that you would have put up with before taking this course?"

* A great teacher—Jesus—once said regarding outcomes assessment: "Judge not that you be not judged!"[7]

* There is no learning outcome in ideas. Kant in the *Critique of Judgment* called the goal of thinking ideas a "purposeless purpose (*Zweckmässigkeit ohne Zweck*)."[8] In this sense every course in arts and

37

ideas is purposeless. Useless, at least in a utilitarian sense. A course in ideas is in a way successful to the extent that expected learning outcomes are iconoclastically deconstructed, i.e., insofar as they are not achieved. As Plato said in the *Meno*: If you know what you are seeking, you are already there and there is no point to the seeking. If you don't know what you are seeking, you might discover something, but you will never know if it was what you were after.[9] There is no way to judge it.

* Imagine the identification of desired learning outcomes written by the chef or by Alice Waters on the menu of Chez Panisse, or announced by the conductor of the Boston Pops in the program notes before a concert, or articulated by a Zen roshi before a two-week sesshin. Try to imagine these and you will see how silly and inappropriate is the attempt to identify desired learning outcomes in the teaching of arts and ideas in any serious educational enterprise.

* The educational institutions that advertise student—or teaching—centeredness aren't. Their faculties are increasingly under pressure to prove and to assess, to name rather than to do. Their eye is off the ball. The students (as students) are losers. The students are not honored as scholars.

* In the ancient world, an important distinction was made between teaching (*didachê*) and preaching (*kêrygma*). The latter is done in a loud voice, as when the herald (*kêrux*) announces the winner at the Olympic games, whereas the former is whispered. Preaching is aimed at outsiders who need conversion, whereas teaching is for those already converted, as in catechetical instruction and debate. Preaching, according to old rabbinic convention, is done while standing, whereas teaching should be done sitting down.[10] So preaching is "standing up for" something and its aim is to convert the student to what the preacher imagines is the true opinion or faith (orthodoxy), while teaching is, so to say, "sitting down into" the matter at hand. Preachers, on this view, can identify desired learning objectives in advance, but teachers cannot. In being asked to identify in advance desired learning objectives and assessing the results thereof, teachers are being asked to be preachers, not real teachers.

A great teacher is one who is empty of preachings and preachments, ego's or society's cherished attitudes, standpoints, and beliefs. In this emptying there can be a resonance, like the empty sound box of a guitar or cello. What resonates are other melodies and harmonies, ideas and values that transcend any particular teacher or teaching. This is why I have said: one desirable learning outcome is not to have a desired learning outcome.

Notes

1 Martin Heidegger, *What is Called Thinking?*, trans. F. D. Wieck and J. G. Gray (New York: Harper, 1968), 118–119.
2 Ludwig Wittgenstein, *Philosophical Investigations*, trans. G. E. M. Anscombe (Oxford: Basil Blackwell, 1958), 115.
3 Eric Partridge, *Origins* (New York: Macmillan, 1959), 124–476.
4 Huston Smith, *The World's Religions* (San Francisco: Harper San Francisco, 1991), 159.
5 Andrew Vogel Ettin, *Speaking Silences: Stillness and Voice in Modern Thought and Jewish Tradition* (Charlottesville: University of Virginia Press, 1994), 183–184.
6 Norman O. Brown, "Apocalypse: The Place of Mystery in the Life of the Mind," in *Interpretation: The Poetry of Meaning*, ed. S. R. Hopper and D. L. Miller (New York: Harcourt Brace and World, 1967), 9.
7 Matt. 7:1.
8 Immanuel Kant, *Critique of Judgment*, trans J. H. Bernard (New York: Hafner Publishing, 1951), 55.
9 Plato, *Meno,* trans. W. R. M. Lamb (Cambridge: Harvard University Press, 1982), 299–301.
10 David L. Miller, *Christs: Meditations of Archetypal Images in Christian Theology* (New York: Seabury Press, 1981), 111–117.

FINDING THE PHILOSOPHER'S STONE

Robin L. Gordon

My philosophy of education has been fairly consistent over the past thirty years, years that have flown by since I first obtained my secondary-teaching credential. I have taught at the college level for many years; however, I still recall my first teenage students whom I taught when I was just out of college and how they could both enchant and annoy me. I loved my content area, science, but intuitively understood that the classroom was peopled with more than the thirty-five adolescents sitting before me. They embodied at least two personalities each, a Dr. Jekyll and Mr. Hyde on a daily basis. For instance, one day they would be carefree young people; the next day they would be devastated and angry over some slight, real or imagined.

I also learned that their enthusiasm for science or any other subject area could not be taken for granted and that young people had challenges in their lives that might take precedence over my lesson on any given day. Thus, as I continued with my own graduate work in education, thinkers such as Carl Rogers, A. S. Neill, Barbara Clark, and Philip Jackson spoke to my own intuition that I needed to make classroom space for both scholarship and soul. Implementing this belief has remained a goal of mine throughout my teaching at the college level.

Experimentation with curriculum and teaching methods was actually encouraged in the secondary classroom in the late 1970s. Tests and accountability were important diagnostic tools for assisting the teacher in making certain her curriculum covered the content deemed important by the State Department of Education. However, there was still occasion for teachers to incorporate areas of special interest within their content area, which allowed us to explore a subject in a deeper and more meaningful way rather than being limited to memorized facts. We had the time to connect ideas across various subject areas and to help students discover how interrelated knowledge is. We also had time to pay attention to our students' stories and to act as witnesses to their soul work. By soul work, I refer to my belief that a significant goal of education is to spend time learning, reflecting, and developing into the person one was meant to be.

One example of the struggle to balance content and soul seems like it occurred ages ago, back when sex education used to be taught as part of a standard life science curriculum. The unit was actually a pleasure to teach because teachers had no difficulty getting the students motivated to pay attention, even if it meant learning the anatomy and physiology of the reproductive system. Yet, teaching sex education challenged us then because adolescents hungered to discuss topics that went beyond the science curriculum. They needed to explore the nature of relationship and what it meant to be responsible. Moral dilemmas emerged that were certainly outside the scope of the textbook. It raised the question: how do teachers allow room for examining deep issues while refraining from imposing their values onto young people who need to develop their own belief systems? My colleagues and I required time to sort out these issues without having an administrator check to see whether we were covering the same page in the textbook.

That dance of soul and ego continued to haunt me as an educator of future teachers seeking their credentials. I recently read an entry in my journal from almost twenty years ago, in which I wrote heatedly after a difficult week with a department chair, "As usual, I worry about sacrificing content; however . . . . they [my education students] have questions outside the curriculum and as I totally disagree with Madeline Hunter's theory[1] as a rigid structure, I believe it is important to address these needs as they arise as long as the class remains focused on goals." My philosophy of education, moreover, did not endear me to many teacher educators at that time!

It troubles me to hear current teachers worry that there is no time for depth in their teaching because they have to cover content that will be assessed on standardized exams. Students are basically tested on the kinds of questions a contestant would be asked on *Jeopardy*, easily answered if one has enough facts stored in the cerebral hard drive. Western education perceives knowledge as something one can gather and store permanently, in contrast to other systems that recognize the ongoing and ever-changing relationship between the learner and knowledge.

After witnessing education rush toward accountability, I concluded that nothing was going to change in the traditional power structure that had become politicized and entrenched in an atmosphere of blaming teachers for its ills. "Teacher-proof" curricula was developed, meaning anyone breathing could teach it. Teacher education programs at the universities became just as mired in the accountability movement. Beginning teachers were evaluated on how well they followed a set lesson plan, and any deviation from the plan to allow for debate or questions raised by students that might move the discussion in a different direction was criticized and labeled "bird walking."

Thus, nearly ten years ago, I began a new journey to the borderland: a study of depth psychology. It was in that study that I reexamined my earlier thoughts about education and how I wanted my teaching to be. My depth work was such a synchronicity: by changing my course, I was able to focus again on important concerns that I had first noticed as a beginning teacher. Furthermore, initiating an exploration of C. G. Jung's work on alchemy was like being given the name for a word one has been trying to recall in that frustrating, tip-of-the-tongue memory game. Alchemy is typically thought of as the old science of turning lead into gold, which is an enormous oversimplification. Jung, however, explored the alchemical operations in a psychological framework in relationship to his individuation theory. Philosophically, I had come full circle and knew that this area of study was home.

I have been studying the field of alchemy for the past seven years; however, unconsciously I have long been aware of this old science that merges spirit and matter. Besides Jung, others who wrote on the parallels between alchemy and psychic development, such as Edward Edinger and Marie-Louise von Franz, have become my guides as well as companions. Furthermore, I have made numerous new friends, from antiquity through the present, while exploring the *Magnum Opus* and deepening my understanding of the sciences I have treasured.

The reason I mention my investigations in alchemy in this essay is this: as I think about my experiences in the classroom, I discover that they parallel what has become a familiar series of alchemical operations. Like the alchemists practicing their art, I have found teaching to be a spiritual exercise or, more accurately, a reflection of my own soul work. This essay does not examine methods for assisting students in achieving higher test scores or even better grades. Those are ego-driven aspects of education that simply brush the surface of learning. Rather, I wish to concentrate on what is less visible but is nevertheless ever so deep, profound, and what makes a classroom seem much more crowded than the number of students would indicate.

Calcinatio

One of the first steps in alchemical work, *calcinatio*, requires fire. The substance that is worked upon in the transmutation process undergoes a period of concentrated burning until it turns to a fine white ash. *Calcinatio* is hot and parched. It is also a focusing operation, reducing material to its basic elements. Teaching has given me the opportunity to witness students undergoing *calcinatio* as well as perceiving this operation in my own growth as an educator. Many years ago, after the death of my first baby earlier that fall, I accepted a position as a long-term substitute for an eighth-grade science class. I was enveloped in my own sorrow and needed to return to the classroom, which had been my sanctuary from childhood.

The previous teacher had gone on sabbatical and, unbeknownst to me, was a freethinker regarding classroom structure. I should first mention that I struggle with wanting the classroom to be a setting for active learning while also realizing that adolescent energy can be overwhelming. Especially in the early days of my career, I wished for students to be able to make choices regarding their education but was not clear on how to achieve it without the classroom tumbling into chaos. Therefore, before this new semester began, I rearranged the classroom in a traditional column and row formation, stood by my desk, and greeted my new students. Thinking back, I sense they must have felt that their own journey into the Underworld had begun. Having grown accustomed to a fun and caring *puer*, they were confronted with the terrible, albeit reluctant, Baba Yaga. I knew I had miscalculated when a rather pleasant and feisty student turned her desk over in a fury.

Fortunately, my nature was really more inclined toward nurturing, such that by the end of the semester, the fire in my classroom had burned out. I recognized, however, that I did not like the taste of ash in my teaching, at least not as a result of my ineptitude. I learned what it was to be the alchemist's bumbling assistant and vowed to do better.

Solutio

Early on in the alchemical process, the Adept places the matter into solution, repeating this step numerous times. It is a wet, dark flood of work. In dream imagery we often experience *solutio* as swimming in the ocean. The unconscious can overwhelm and dissolve ego, which is both frightening as well as enlightening if one has the courage to keep swimming. Tears fall— the concretization of *solutio*, which is often healing, sometimes expressions of fierce anger and frustration and, just as often, of celebration and joy.

It is not unusual for teachers of adolescents to be confronted with tears. Teenagers have such deeply felt highs as well as lows. One minute they would tumble into class, excitedly telling me of some adventure. The next minute, I would get sullen looks after asking for quiet. It is unfortunate that some educators dismiss the intensity of adolescent angst as being manipulative and inauthentic. Our students are working out what kind of adults they will be, and they need their teachers to create a containing place in which they can toil. Yet, policy makers as well as parents have been blinded by an obsession with achieving ever-increasing test scores. Above-average is not enough.

Teachers are neither psychotherapists nor drones. During my tenure at another middle school, one of my fairly consistent students began to fall apart academically. When he told me that his baby brother had died, he did not need an academic pep talk; he needed to cry and to be comforted, not by a bureaucrat but by a caring human being.

Unlike many teachers in the secondary education system today, I find that, as a professor in a college that stresses the importance of good teaching, I have the freedom to encourage academic rigor while still taking time to attend to students' stories. Adult learners are often overflowing with tales of upheaval that come with grown-up life. Their experiences need to be spoken and heard. These elders-in-the making have their tears, and my gift is to be able to listen as a witness to their sorrow. Yes, I have a syllabus that needs to be covered, and yet students must also learn to balance their requirements for scholarship with the plethora of disruptions inevitable in their lives.

Sublimatio

The *sublimatio* operation may be more familiar to the modern thinker as distillation. In this stage of alchemy, the solution is heated until the vital elements are gathered in a vapor that makes a skyward journey before being deposited in a collecting flask. Fortunately, brilliance and flying above the clouds also finds a place in the classroom and, in fact, must occur or teachers would burn out in far greater numbers than they do. A common joy expressed by teachers occurs when their students work through a difficult concept and then "the light bulb goes on, and they get it!" My current teacher-education students become elated as they describe a lesson that has gone well, one in which they have skillfully guided students in discovering a new concept.

It may be easy for those who have not taught to underestimate the feeling of excitement that accompanies a well-executed lesson effective in reaching its goals. For example, I developed a demonstration lesson for my teacher candidates that involves pirates and whole-brain learning. I have as much fun as my students, not just because the activity is entertaining (despite my inability to master pirate-speak) but also because it teaches the concept so well. Ahhh *sublimatio*—so sweet; yet we know that what goes up must come down.

Coagulatio

Upon spending a requisite amount of time in the waters of *solutio*, the material must now congeal or coagulate, collecting at the bottom of the flask. After the delight of *sublimatio*, it is actually a relief to feel the gravitas of *coagulatio*. When psychological material becomes discernable, it can be worked upon. One needs to be able to hold the material, turn it over, and observe it from all angles in order to make sense of how it came to be in this place and how it should be integrated into psyche. When psychic materials are residing solely in the unconscious, they are ethereal and immune to reflection. Thus, *coagulatio* is a time for contemplation and deepening of ideas. No matter how brilliant my lesson seems, I find that meditation uncovers new things to consider, new areas to explore.

Reflecting in a journal about my teaching day often creates epiphanies for me. One year I had a particularly challenging class—5th period, the period right before lunch! For those who have taught secondary students, one only needs to name the class period as a noun and roll one's eyes to elicit sympathy from colleagues. Early in the year, 5th period was challenging my authority, and one day students actually stopped class five minutes early to socialize. I had never experienced anything like it and was dumbfounded. Rather than throw a tantrum, I stood quietly until they left the classroom for lunch. I then sat on the floor where no one could see me and dissolved into tears. Having experienced a cleansing, I could then sit and ponder how I had come to this place and how I would proceed. I also wrote in my journal and--*coagulatio* occurred. I reorganized my thinking, and the class was back on track the next day. I realized I had not taken into account that this group needed much more containment in the form of classroom procedures than I had been giving; once I provided it, there was never a repeat of the mutiny. One of the students I had wanted to remove from that class concluded the year by telling me, "I never thought I would miss you—but I will!" I had the same thought.

The reflective cycle of teaching is so critical and yet often so lacking for elementary and secondary teachers. How amazing and what a joy to have time to think about one's practice and then to modify it to better match one's goals and intentions. Lip service is paid by administrators regarding the need for reflective practice, but the factory mentality of education leaves no time for such a valuable exercise. It is not solely the fault of administration either, but rather a by-product of the current culture of American education.

Mortificatio

Creating the Philosopher's Stone requires that there be a period of time when elements are allowed to putrefy and decompose. Literal death and disintegration are perhaps too commonly encountered by teachers, not only in urban schools but also in those communities who have experienced natural or human-generated disasters. Personal grief or tragedies such as those that took place at Columbine High School and Virginia Tech can devastate teachers as they try to make sense of what has gone wrong in the educational system. However, like the Tarot card for death, I would like to speak about this aspect of both teaching and alchemy in its necessary and positive aspect. One must go through death before rebirth.

I enjoy using Plato's "Allegory of the Cave" in one of my teacher-education classes as a basis for discussion and reflection. However, Plato's discourse on the purpose of education raises a significant ethical question: if we accept that the teacher's role is to assist the learner in turning from the inner cave toward the light, are we also prepared to be guides as well as witnesses to our students when life turns them toward the dark? And should we occasionally turn them toward the dark ourselves?

I am thinking of a graduate student who was a devout Christian. In the course of a discussion on student self-esteem, I mentioned the importance of our shadow. I worried that I might trouble this young man whose religious upbringing included the shadow's repression. This example illustrates two aspects of teaching that I take seriously. First, one of my charges is to raise questions that will challenge students' beliefs and preconceptions. However, I also believe that when I invite *mortificatio* into the classroom, it must be done with great care and respect. Some of my students are not ready for a descent into Hades and I have no right to force them on a journey for which they are unprepared. W. H. Auden's last lines in "Funeral Blues" expresses this caution:

The stars are not wanted now: put out every one;
Pack up the moon and dismantle the sun;
Pour away the ocean and sweep up the wood;
For nothing now can ever come to any good.[2]

Auden's expressed grief is at a level often encountered in the adolescent as well as in the college student. As a teacher, I can act as witness and provide encouragement when needed.

Separatio

During the alchemical process, once the matter has decayed it is put back into solution and distilled to separate the corrupted matter from the uncorrupted. Psychologically, *separatio* is a growing sense of opposing elements in the psyche. For example, both men and women carry the feminine and masculine principles, yin and yang. Our work is to achieve a palpable harmony between dualities, such as those that emerge in parent/child or teacher/student relationships.

Separatio has two connotations for me as a teacher. Some students concretize the use of the sword in the sorting out process that takes place in the adolescent years. They use razor blades and scissors on their bodies to ease the anxiety of feelings that are unbearable, or so they seem to the untutored. That is *separatio* as an extreme, injurious, and literalized practice. However, there is another wonderfully positive, albeit trying, aspect to this stage in psychic work. One of the tasks of adolescence is to separate from one's parents and other adults, to find out who *I* am, which is not *they*. The process of *separatio* can cause intense anxiety for the young person, which may be further exacerbated by the frustrated adult who has seen those eyes roll one too many times.

Before I had my own children, I would tell my female students who were behaving particularly irritably on a particular day to "save it for their mothers." I am sure there is a trickster spirit out there who clapped his hands upon hearing my words, anticipating a day when one of my own teenage children, upon watching me drink water from a kitchen faucet, looked at me with the disdain that only a teen can muster and confessed: "You make me sick!" She could not believe I could be so uncouth, and I am sure at a deeper level her containing-mother vessel fractured.

Separatio can cause immense angst in the midst of necessary rebellion. The adult's role is to psychically contain young people in the process while they do their work. I do not mean to say we accept disrespect; now as an adult, my daughter expressed some discomfort when I joked about the faucet story. However, I also reminded her that she rarely acted out teenage anxiety and that I was actually relieved she could say what she did, although I certainly did not mention it at the time! Once I became a parent, I understood better how to act as a container for my students' (and my own children's) anxiety. I did not have to react to their *separatio* statements as a peer but, rather, as a guide and mentor. I hope I made up for my original rash language as one who was uninitiated.

Coniunctio

Individuation is a term used to describe the ongoing development of the psyche. Jung explains that the goal of individuation is to bring opposite psychic qualities, the conscious and the unconscious, into relationship with each other to form a union, what he called the transcendent function.[3] Individuation is a lifelong process; however, people who actively seek this path begin to sense a calming and authentic wisdom as they travel in the course of their lives. Unification is also the goal of the alchemical process characterized by the *coniunctio* phase, in which the elements, symbolized by Sol and Luna or male and female, are recombined to create the Philosopher's Stone. The alchemists believed that the feminine and masculine principles in matter needed to be purified separately before they could be joined in *coniunctio*. Psychologically, one examines one's complexes and neuroses in order to integrate unconscious contents into the psyche in a healthy way. The alchemists observed that the combination of substances formed a new, third ingredient, also called the Philosophical Child. Thus, the alchemical marriage requires holding opposite qualities in harmony.

One of my favorite *coniunctio* teacher stories concerns a class of eighth grade honors students I had the pleasure of teaching at a school in a neighborhood with considerable gang problems. One day they expressed the ubiquitous teenage complaint: "This is boring!" Although there may have been a touch of sarcasm in my answer, I challenged them to try teaching the class. The students were ahead in their content, so I felt comfortable offering them one day a week to prepare a lesson on anything science-oriented. I then stepped back and let them take over the class. Four students took on the challenge and taught their peers. One young man who teetered on the verge of getting into trouble taught his lesson with more confidence and poise than some of my former student-teachers. My principal, an effective progressive educator, sat in on the class, enjoying the experience of seeing one of her students finding his voice. The young man even sent one of his classmates out into the hall for talking too much. I don't know whether he went on to become a teacher, but that day I had the privilege of watching a young person in his transition to adulthood, an event that transcends testing.

I am not convinced that *coniunctio* (in this case, the coniunctio of student and teacher) happens often in the classroom. First, with the current emphasis on high test scores as the goal of education, there is little time to cover the inordinate amount of content that is found in American textbooks. Second, balancing the needs of soul in one's classroom can leave much unfinished work at semester's end, certainly something to be frowned upon by administrators who are accountable to both parents and the state education system. I may feel that by May I have achieved my goal of creating a seed of *coniunctio*; however, I do not often see transmutation take place. That is a private affair, although occasionally I receive reports from my former students regarding their continued explorations and experiences. These lovely stories and cherished notes of gratitude are immeasurable gifts that help me know whether my alchemical practice is accurate or needs adjusting. I mention this not to gratify my ego but to support something I often tell my teacher-education students: never underestimate your potential for doing both good and harm.

Conclusion

I hope my words convey how soulful an experience teaching has been and remains for me. Teaching, like alchemy, is a rough-and-tumble work. It requires the Adept to experiment, to be creative, and to continue to learn. There is so much more to the practice of teaching than assisting students to achieve high test scores. Many colleges have become little more than vocational schools, with the main question from students being, "What job can I get when I graduate?" As elders in education, we should remind our students, our student-teachers, and the culture at large that although a job is very important, as we age and grow wiser we learn that the needs of soul are indeed the most essential for happiness.

Teaching is a work in progress in which even master teachers who have journeyed far continue to evolve, grow, and deepen their practice. Teaching has changed me in ways that are too numerous to include in this essay. The alchemists believed that it takes more than one lifetime to find the Philosopher's Stone. I take heart in this belief and continue to work at my vocation.

Recently, a synchronicity took place for me as I began to conclude this essay. My teaching style reflects all the experiences and reflections I have had teaching so many types of students, from prekindergarten and secondary through graduate school. What I can only consider a gift from the universe came to me a few days after I had a disagreement regarding effective teaching process with a respected colleague who had a different teaching style than I. Two students approached me on different days to thank me for teaching their class. They wanted me to know that they were beginning to understand the complexities of the content and were grateful to me for helping them achieve a fulfilling sense of confidence, which I liken to finding the Philosopher's Stone. And there it was, my own Philosopher's Stone, evident in my teaching and found at last.

Notes

[1] Madeline Hunter was a leading educational theorist for many years whose *7 Step Lesson Plan* was used by a large number of administrators to evaluate teachers and to criticize those who followed different lesson plan models.

[2] W. H. Auden, "Funeral Blues," in *Collected Poems* (New York: Vintage Books, 1991).

[3] C. G. Jung, in *The Essential Jung*, ed. A. Storr (Princeton: Princeton University Press, 1999).

RESTORING SOUL TO TEACHING: REFLECTIONS ON THE DIVISION OF SPIRIT FROM MATTER IN TEACHING AND LEARNING

Betty J. Mceady

Balancing the scales
Restoring spirit to matter
The whole completed
Made cosmic again.
~Marimba Ani[1]

Marimba Ani argues in her book, *Yurugu*, that Plato's compartmentalization of "reason," "appetite" and "emotion" represents one of the most problematical divisions in European thought and behavior.[2] Giving primacy to reason over emotion has led to the "splitting of the human being. No longer whole, we later become Descartes' mind versus body. The superiority of the intellectual over the emotional self has led to the separation of spirit from matter."[3] This same dichotomy prevails in aspects of education today in American society.

Compelled by the loss of wholeness and spirit in teaching due to "The Elementary and Secondary Education Act of 2001"[4]—or "The No Child Left Behind Act"—some educators are seeking ways to balance the scales in hopes of restoring soul to teaching. In light of this division of reason from emotion, implicative of The No Child Left Behind Act, I wish to reflect on the effects of the separation of spirit and soul from rationality in teaching and learning. While the wording of the act communicates a vision of a solid education for all children and youth, many of its alleged implementations have generally missed the mark. On the contrary, from these practices has arisen an ominous loss of vitality and wholeness in a profession in which the sum total of individual achievement and action affects the quality of life of this nation and, because of the global interests and involvements of the United States, perchance the world. Teaching and learning are social fuel in the progress and power of a society.

As I reflect on the current consciousness of teachers and teacher educators in public schools and universities across the nation, particularly under the throes of the No Child Left Behind Act, I recall expressions and lamentations of loss of spirit and soul in teaching—a "paradise lost." Teacher candidates in my classrooms who seek a breath of hope have asked: "Since you have been teaching for a long time and have seen a lot of changes, do you think—as other educational fads have come and gone—that this focus on tests, standards, and prescriptive teaching will also disappear?" "How long do you think No Child Left Behind will last?" These questions from preservice teachers are undeniable signs of soul disaffection among potentially good teachers, a disaffection fueled by the excessive focus by external authorities on a one-dimensional approach to education. Similar questions continue to come forth from teacher education classrooms across the nation. John Goodlad describes a parallel experience:

> Their concerns spilled forth: Was there any hope that this overriding preoccupation with tests might soon end? Their frustrations were still on my mind when I settled down one evening with *The Art of the Commonplace*, by Wendell Berry. The book cautioned about the dangers of local matters of daily life coming under the control of distant "expert" bureaucracies, making them "world problems" requiring "world solutions," taking over from the people intimately familiar with the circumstances. This usurpation of local intelligence is colonizing many domains of modern life.[5]

Soul and Teaching

The meaning of soul, according to archetypal psychologist James Hillman, "is best given by its context. . . . human behavior is understandable because it has an inside meaning. The inside meaning is suffered and experienced."[6] Although soul in this context is the analyst's metaphor for inner human experience, soul as used in other contexts inclines toward a perspective of inner depth, existing independently of human experience. For example, a black poetess of the early twentieth century, Priscilla J.

Thompson, describes soul as "the inner realm," "the secret sphere," and "a sacred realm shut in from sight" by other humankind,[7] one that holds the secrets of each person's lived and imagined experience.

Hillman reminds us of other words associated with soul, although the meaning in each case varies with context and purpose: "mind, spirit, heart, life, warmth, humanness, personality, individuality, intentionality, essence, innermost purpose, emotion, quality, virtue, morality, sin, wisdom, death, God."[8] No matter the context, soul is perceived as the intangible, elusive, and indefinable depths of a physical form (animate and inanimate). He amplifies his meaning of soul by attributing to it three characteristics:

First, *soul* refers to the *deepening* of events into experiences; second, the significance *soul* makes possible, whether in love or in religious concern, derives from its special *relation with death*. And third, by *soul* I mean the imaginative possibility in our natures, the experiencing through reflective speculation, dream, image, and *fantasy*—that mode which recognizes all realities as primarily symbolic or metaphorical.[9]

Hillman, as he later clarifies, is constructing a psychology of soul based on "the processes of imagination . . . a *poetic basis of mind*."[10] It is his third quality of soul that is the central context of this paper. It is the teacher's loss of imaginative possibility, reflective speculation, and soul-making that has resulted in a dispirited disposition towards public school teaching. I attribute such bewilderment to excessive legislative impositions upon teachers regarding classroom matters. When teachers, including teacher educators, are forced into one-dimensional and robotic instructional practices, then their imaginative potentialities are thwarted, if not demeaned. Thus, I propose to restore spirit (or soul) to the matter of teaching, which includes a concern for methods, techniques, and processes. I conclude this essay by considering the integration of spiritual instructional aids in teaching according to archetypal pedagogies, especially those that are spiritually and culturally responsive, based on a model of *educare*.

Loss of Heart and Soul in Teaching and Learning

Public school teachers and teacher educators are experiencing a loss of heart: beginning teachers are discouraged virtually before they enter the profession; many veteran teachers are on the edge, enduring but not enjoying teaching. Because a preponderance of demands by external authorities (state legislators, educational bureaucracies, etc.) elevate high-stakes testing and the use of one-dimensional goals and methods of instruction over learner-centeredness and culturally-responsive curricula, many teachers are left bereft of their penchant for the kind of creativity that best serves their respective learners. In many instances, teachers' continued employment, compensation, or promotion opportunities are threatened if their students fail to demonstrate certain levels of achievement on standardized tests. Oftentimes, expectations of student achievement at higher levels of performance within the regular academic year are unrealistic—particularly in the cases of middle and high school students who have been "left behind" since their first day in poor-performing public schools. Poorly-funded schools breed "savage inequalities"[11] and pressure already conscientious students to become pathologically concerned about "passing the test."

Although external authorities, such as state legislators and educational policymakers, should address equitable and appropriate funding for all schools, they instead choose to focus on day-to-day activities—such as classroom teaching—that have little relevance to their roles and responsibilities as policymakers. Meanwhile, inequitable funding on both the state and national levels renders poor schools poorer while destroying teachers' inclinations to teach creatively. These same inequities lead inevitably to teacher shortages, disaffected teachers, and teachers misassigned to teach subjects for which they have engaged in little or no content preparation. Similarly, funding inequities foster schools that are culturally irresponsive and therefore tend to miseducate our children and youth.

This loss of soul is complex and tragic. James Hillman believes that "we can and do lose our souls."[12] He describes a psychotherapeutic episode that holds parallel implications for teachers who have lost (or are losing) their heart and spirit:

One day in Burghölzli, the famous institute in Zurich where the words *schizophrenia* and *complex* were born, I watched a woman being interviewed. She sat in a wheelchair because she was elderly and feeble. She said that she was dead for she had lost her heart. The psychiatrist asked her to place her hand over her breast to feel her heart beating: it must still be there if she could feel its beat. "That," she said, "is not my real heart." She and the psychiatrist looked at each other. There was nothing more to say. . . . she had lost the loving courageous connection to life—and that is the real heart, not the ticker which can as well pulsate isolated in a glass bottle.[13]

Similarly, high-stakes testing has taken on pathological and punitive characteristics, with mathathanic effects (Fr. *mathanein*: to learn; Gk. *Thanatos*: akin to death; thus the tendency to kill the spirit of learning) on students and disquieting effects on teachers. In other words, the hearts of the teachers and students are ticking but these are not their real hearts. Their real hearts reflect an authentic connectedness to their students, to their subject/content, to themselves, and to a global society. Teachers and students are losing their souls—particularly in inner-city and rural schools—to the overwhelming and singled-minded focus on technique, content, and process. Creativity, cultural responsiveness, learner-centeredness, and spirituality are in absentia—not as in playing hooky but locked out and left at the threshold of the classroom door.

The Absence of Soul: Like a "Paradise Lost"

> . . . apte the Mind or Fancie is to roave
> Uncheckt, and of her roaving is no end;
> Till warn'd, or by experience taught, she learn
> That not to know at large of things remote
> From use, obscure and suttle, but to know
> That which before us lies in daily life,
> Is the prime Wisdom, what is more, is fume,
> Or emptiness, or fond impertinence,
> And renders us in things that most concerne
> Unpractis'd, unprepar'd, and still to seek.
> Therefore from the high pitch let us descend
> A lower flight, and speak of things at hand
> Useful. . .

John Milton[14]

This excerpt from Milton's *Paradise Lost* has poetic considerations for the distant expert bureaucracies that tend to exercise control over the daily matters of classroom teaching. Bureaucrats or policymakers, as Milton's poem might be interpreted, must learn "that not to know at large of things remote/From use, obscure and suttle, is the prime Wisdom"; otherwise, external authorities, because they are remote from the classroom, have a tendency to impose repressive legislation and mandates upon teachers, students, and administrators who are intimately involved in the learning process. The suggestion here is that the mind of the bureaucrat roves ceaselessly unchecked over the daily classroom instructional responsibilities of teachers—with a dispiriting effect on most teachers' efforts to connect holistically with their students. Impertinence and irrelevance result from the actions of external experts. Allegedly to "leave no child behind," these external authorities (bureaucracies) instead disrupt the business and spirit of teaching, making teaching emotionally more difficult than ever and exacerbating inherent challenges in teaching and learning. Ultimately, those children/learners who were left behind prior to the 2001 legislation are left even further behind today, as they are tested repeatedly until they are coerced into a cognitive stupor, threatened with grade retention or with lack of high school certification, and their already low self-esteem exacerbated by hopelessness of ever passing "the test."

On the other hand, not only is there is a message for legislators and bureaucrats in this excerpt from *Paradise Lost*, there is also a message for teachers and teacher candidates to consider. Since teachers are intimately involved with and knowledgeable about their students, including awareness of their daily learning needs and efforts, it is teachers' moral obligation to look within for spiritual aids to teach creatively. Carrying forward such a mission of care and social justice is in counteraction to forces that tend—albeit inadvertently—to kill the spirit of creative teaching and learning. The split intrinsic to external policymakers between cognition and emotion, process and spirit, does not have to characterize teachers' learner-centered approaches to teaching and learning. Standards and external authorities do not stifle teachers' creativity unless teachers choose to surrender it.

Teachers could (perhaps must) use state standards to frame their instructional portraits of day-to-day teaching and learning within their respective classrooms. Mary Oliver in her poem "The Journey" proffers a similar message: "One day you finally knew what you had to do, and began."[15] Teachers must begin to appeal to soul companionship to find the gift that is the archetypal image of who they are and then discern which gifts they can bring forward to serve themselves and learners.

Restoring Spirit to Matter: An Ethical Responsibility of Educators

Although the first section of this essay may seem highly critical of the emphasis on process and technique so intrinsic to most educational policies and accountability legislation, I hold much respect for process and strategies in teaching. The problem, as I have described, is the excessive emphasis on factual cognition and mastery of technique to the exclusion of emotional and spiritual ways of knowing and learning. My intent is to highlight an element that is often missing in educational policies and accountability legislation and consequently in teacher education and teacher development. As Marimba Ani proclaims in "Incantations," I recommend "balancing the scales,"[16] restoring spirit to teaching and learning processes.

The convergence of spirit and matter is a developing interest of 21st century neurobiologists and metaphysical researchers as they investigate connections between spiritual (including religious) experience and brain functions. Is the mind (conscious and unconscious) merely a construction of cerebral functions, or does it exist in its own archetypal realm, independent of the brain? At this time, I don't know whether neurobiologists can tell us more than merely the locus of brain functions during a spiritual experience. My penchant for a synergistic perspective leads me to suggest an interdependence of spirit and matter. My perspective is influenced by Egyptian cosmology, a "Doctrine of the Soul" that holds body and soul as one, "not two distinct things, but one in two different aspects; the soul is the power which a living body possesses, and it is the end for which the body exists, the final cause of its existence."[17]

Similarly, because the learner brings mind, body, and soul as *one* to the learning setting, I value teaching and learning approaches that address learners as the whole beings that they are, rather than as simply automatons who merely need to master isolated sets of facts, techniques, and skills as proof of achievement. Our nation's schools—perhaps our nation in general, I dare say—need what Anthony Storr calls a *metanoia* experience: a rebirth of the spirit, a regeneration of the individual and perchance of the society.[18] Whenever social conditions are a result of "all the thinking and looking after" occurring at the top, and all dimensions of accountability are left to a higher political and social authority, then the freedom of the individual turns into spiritual and physical slavery.[19] This colonization of individual psyches eclipses individual creativity, action, reflection, and transformation. Forcing teachers to follow merely the decisions and prescriptive methods of higher authorities and policymakers is antithetical to an education born out of a praxis of creative reflection, action, and transformation. "It is absolutely essential that the oppressed participate in the revolutionary process with an increasingly critical awareness of their role as Subjects of the transformation."[20]

Jungian psychologists tell us that cultural forms and practices reveal much about both the individual and the collective psyche. Edward F. Edinger posits that culture and religion mirror the psyche, and in addition to cultural forms reflecting who we are, the psyche has an "ethical element" and a responsibility to community/society.[21] It is the ethical responsibility of educators (including teachers, teacher educators, and policymakers) to the individual and society to connect the psychic and material realms in the education process. Parker Palmer supports this convergence of spirit and matter when he writes: "Reduce teaching to intellect, and it becomes a cold abstraction; reduce it to emotions, and it becomes narcissistic; reduce it to the spiritual, and it loses its anchor to the world."[22] Palmer calls for the convergence of the "intellectual" (the way we think about teaching and how people know and learn), the "emotional" (the feelings and archetypal interactions between teacher and student), and the "spiritual" (the diverse ways we connect our hearts with our work, our students, our personal interactions, and ourselves).[23]

Heart and Soul as Poetic Basis for Good Teaching

Good teachers possess a capacity for connectedness. They are able to weave a complex web of connections among themselves, their subjects, and their students, so that students can learn to weave a world for themselves. . . . . The connections made by good teachers are held not in their methods but in their hearts—the place where intellect and emotion and spirit will converge in the human self.[24]

I have read Parker Palmer's *The Courage to Teach* several times and assuredly will read it repeatedly over my lifetime. It reminds me—at each reading—of the moment I realized that my confidence level as an educator grew stronger when I connected care of my soul (spiritual perspective) with care of and relationship with my teacher candidates (my students). My determination to help them connect to the world of teaching is by integrating the technical, emotional, and spiritual aspects of the profession.

Palmer's adage that "we teach who we are" awakened my self-knowledge and awareness of my own transformation from education to *educare*. The Latin root of education, *educare* means to think and draw out information from within. Sri Sathya Sai Baba asserts: "Education is for a living while *educare* is for life."[25] Thus, by focusing on improvement of my spiritual character, I also recognize my moral responsibility to motivate teacher candidates to look within for their gifts and use these to enhance their teaching. Integrating technique and spirit in teaching gives primacy to transforming education into *educare*.

Education and *Educare*: The Fusion of Matter and Spirit in Teaching

Balancing the scales
Restoring spirit to matter
The whole completed
Made cosmic again.

Education is necessary for a living; *educare* is for life. Both are necessary for restoring balance to matter and spirit in teaching and learning. *E* + *ducere* means to "draw out" or "lead forth." *Educare* teaching methods aim to draw out information from within the learner. They foster multiple dimensions of teaching and learning methods, thus enhancing the possibility of drawing out human potentiality across different realms: cognitive, affective, psychomotor, symbolic, relational, and spiritual. The souls of the learner and the teacher are central in the fusion of spirit and matter in teaching.

How might we begin to approach this fusion in education? Krishnamurti suggests that "education can be transformed only by educating the educator, and not merely creating a new pattern, a new system of action."[26] He further encourages teaching and learning from multidimensional perspectives, in contrast to one-dimensional, technical pedagogies. "Most of us learn technique but have very little to say . . . . We have all the instruments of discovery, without finding anything directly."[27]

In her work on womanist spiritual and liberation ethics, Katie Cannon discusses a teaching perspective that she calls "teaching the womanist idea through metalogues and dialogues."[28] Addressing specifically her approach to teaching, she says: "I too have learned to come to class not thinking of a territory to be covered but with a compass to point the metalogical direction for community of critically conscious ethicists."[29] By creating a virtual community of ethical thinkers in the classroom who generate both consensual and oppositional discussions, Cannon's *educare* approach to teaching promises to bring forth or bring out a higher order of human consciousness in our students.

Reynolds and Piirto describe a soul-based approach to higher order processing as having reverent as well as shadow qualities.[30] From a reverent view, soul-based teaching and learning is about "contemplation; reflection; intuition; metacognition; knowing the true, the beautiful, and the just; dreaming, and imagining with arts-based, philosophical, ethical and social justice curricula that feature a capacity for sufficient depth and complexity."[31] From a shadow view of soul-based teaching and learning "comes a foundation that holds a mature respect for the darker side of human nature."[32] In other words, "good teachers" who are capable of connecting with learners can expect to encounter aspects of their traumas, mental illnesses, physical disorders, fears, neuroses—in sum, their pathologies. The soul exists independently of the human experience but at the same time plays a critical role in forming it. This is consistent with Hillman's depiction of soul as also containing the shadow or the dark realm of individual experience. As such, it is often associated with death, darkness, and separation. The No Child Left Behind Act and its implicative mandates for a cognitive-only approach to teaching ignore the synergy of the reverent and shadow qualities of teaching. Skill and time, not measurable by standardized tests, are at a premium in working with the tension between these two qualities in teaching.

An *educare* approach fosters understanding of both the light and darkness of the soul. For educators this means having the capabilities and connectivity to perceive progress and breakdowns in teaching and learning, whether in the curricula, the learner, or the teacher. Reynolds and Piirto say it quite well:

> Creativity is not always friendly: it is not all light, warm and fuzzy activities infused into content lessons; it is not described by lines and charts; it is not putting on silly costumes and telling jokes; it is not self-esteem exercises, nor fluency and other cognitive divergent production exercises.[33]

In my own experience as a teacher educator, I have learned that creative teaching—teaching that fuses soul and matter—does not guarantee error-free teaching; it does not guarantee excellent student evaluations of teacher or professor performance. There are times when the majority of students (teacher candidates, included) will not understand or be open to the teacher's creative approach. In turn, teacher candidates, for example, must learn that they will have unexpected moments of relational mistakes with their students, ineffective application of strategies, and other disruptions that may seem ominous at times. Such manifestations of the darker side of soul demand only that the teacher attend to the breakdowns and recognize that when the educational process is pathologizing, the soul is calling for redirection and deepening of the process.

I also have learned to value an *educare* approach to teacher training, to acknowledge my teacher candidates' cognitive and emotional learning needs, and to expect some relational or instructional mistakes on my part. For example, my repertoire of research-based (and I must add, state-sanctioned) strategies and techniques in content comprehension and literacy development is extensive. Instead of proffering a litany of strategies, I begin each class session encouraging each candidate to share his or her memorable teaching success and failure of the day or week. It is a checking-in process that acknowledges teacher candidates' current emotional state and also provides a context for me to connect certain teaching strategies to candidates' immediate teaching needs. Together we work out or bring forth possible solutions that they are willing to try in their own teaching situations.

My efforts to fuse cognition (or content) and affect have not always resulted in positive student evaluations (or feedback). Therefore, I find feedback like the following statement from a teacher candidate quite regenerative and encouraging:

Dear Dr. McEady,

Your guidance has been a saving grace this year to all of us in the Single Subject English cohort. In the . . . Capstone presentations, your class and instruction was pointed to by each presenter as the inspiration for some of the best practices, practices that meld with who we and our students are. I look forward to implementing more of the strategies and concepts . . . in next year's teaching.

Of course, as a forty-year veteran teacher, I could present multiple examples of successes and failures in my efforts to employ *educare* teaching methods, but that would extend this essay to an unnecessary length. What is most valuable in the above summative statement is the sentence: "Your . . . instruction was the inspiration for some of the best practices, practices that meld who we and our students are." The implications here are threefold. The teacher candidates found the best practices or strategies that I taught them to be quite helpful and applicable in their respective student teaching. Second, the candidates appreciated my efforts to connect their cognitive learning—their learning of technique—with their emotional needs. And third, my fusion of their cognitive and affective learning needs contributed to their inclination to connect emotionally with the learning needs of their respective middle and high school students. Education and *educare*—the fusion of matter and spirit in teaching—can enhance the value of technical learning and thereby, as Marimba Ani suggests, make the "whole complete" and "cosmic again."[34]

Fusion of Cognitive and Spiritual Dimensions: Promise or Fantasy?

The promise of fusion of spirit and matter in teaching and learning lies not only in my own past experience as a high school and college educator but also in the literature on transformative teaching and scientific studies of mind-matter relations. For this essay, I have drawn upon three excellent texts that espouse the promise of restoring spirit to matter in teaching. Researchers and writers such as Parker Palmer, Elizabeth Tisdell,[35] and Clifford Mayes[36] contend that it is possible to design teaching and learning processes and environments that acknowledge spiritual and archetypal dimensions along with cognitive dimensions (facts, data, information, etc.) of learning and thus be potentially transformational. The following approaches—deliberately shortened for this essay—represent a summary of suggestions from these three authors. They contend that approaches to fusing matter and spirit in teaching and learning should:

- emphasize self-understanding (know thyself) as a teacher; teaching, learning, and knowing in community;
- explore the cognitive (facts, data, information, technical rationality, etc.), affective, relational, symbolic, and intuitive ways of knowing;
- include culturally responsive readings, content, and experiential resources;
- adhere to perspectives that difference and diversity are instruments of excellence;
- concentrate on imagination and creativity as means to making meaning of new information; and
- deploy pedagogies that engage learners in multidimensional ways of knowing while also attending to the archetypal continuum between teacher and learner and teacher as evolving spirit.

Additionally, researchers in depth psychology—a field that acknowledges the continuous interaction of conscious and unconscious influences on human behavior—as well as researchers in the natural sciences are also studying natural and social processes for promising manifestations of mind-matter relations. The unity of matter and spirit is no longer seen as fantasy in the natural sciences. For example, the growing research in quantum physics, neuroscience, neurobiology, and epigenetics (the study of the power of environmental factors on human behavior over and above the effects of genes) along with other scientific studies of mind-matter relations have profound implications for ways of teaching that fuse matter and spirit.

Poetic Conclusion: The Journey and Compost

Mary Oliver's poetic insight highlights my reflections in this essay and defines metaphorically the inner journey of teachers who decide, despite accountability mandates, to balance cognitive and spiritual dimensions in teaching.

One day you finally knew what you had to do, and began,
Though the voices around you kept shouting their bad advice—

. . . .

But you didn't stop.

Mary Oliver"[37]

One day we as teachers and lifelong learners have to decide, despite externally imposed standards and accountability mandates, to take ownership of our respective instructional settings. It is our moral obligation to look within for spiritual aids to teach creatively in order to carry forward a mission of care, social justice, and cognitive dimensions of learning in our classrooms. Oliver's "new voice" is our own voice for creativity, cultural responsiveness, and the fusion of rational, technical, emotional, and spiritual learning in teaching.

Standards, assessment, and accountability are part and parcel of good teaching. As we delve deeper into the soul of teaching, we come to understand the primacy of teaching as complex interactive processes with goals of serving the whole individual as well as society and, ultimately, the world. Perhaps the No Child Left Behind Act and similar external mandates have inadvertently become the "compost"[38] that fertilizes the educational soil for the restoration of soul to teaching. Balancing matter and spirit in teaching and learning has shown up in time and has landed in the perfect compost. It certainly has stellar potential for making the cosmos whole again.

Notes

[1] Marimba Ani, "Incantation," http://www.assatashakur.org/forum/afrikan-traditional-languages-philosophy-worldview/8664-philosophies-marimba-ani-4.html (accessed July 10, 2007).

[2] Marimba Ani, *Yurugu* (Trenton, NJ: Africa World Press, 1994).

³ Ibid., 32.

⁴ "The Elementary and Secondary Education Act of 2001," http://www.ed.gov/policy/elsec/leg/esea02/index.html (accessed July 15, 2007).

⁵ John Goodland, "John Milton's 'Paradise Lost Book VIII'" in *Teaching with Fire: Poetry that Sustains the Courage to Teach*, ed. M. Intrator and M. Scribner (San Francisco: Jossey-Bass, 2003), 48.

⁶ James Hillman, "The Poetic Basis of Mind," in *A Blue Fire: Selected Writings by James Hillman*, ed. T. Moore (New York: Harper & Row , 1989), 19.

⁷ Priscilla Thompson, "Ethiope Lays: Inner Realm," in *Collected Black Women's Poetry*, ed. J. R. Sherman (New York: The Schomburg Library of Nineteenth-Century Black Women Writers, 1900), 18–20.

⁸ James Hillman, *A Blue Fire*, 19.

⁹ Ibid., 21.

¹⁰ Ibid., 22.

¹¹ Jonathan Kozol, *Savage Inequalities: Children in America's Schools* (New York: HarperPerennial, 1991).

¹² James Hillman, *A Blue Fire*, 18.

¹³ Ibid.

¹⁴ John Milton, *Paradise Lost*, http://en.wikisource.org/wiki/Paradise_Lost/Book_VIII (accessed July 26, 2007).

¹⁵ Mary Oliver, "The Journey," *Dream Work* (New York: Atlantic Monthly Press, 1983), 35.

¹⁶ Marimba Ani, "Incantation."

¹⁷ A. Shakur, "Yorubic Medicine: The Art of Divine Herbology" (1990), http://www.assatashakur.org/forum/showthread.php?p=47027, 12 (accessed July 20, 2007).

¹⁸ Anthony Storr, ed., *The Essential Jung* (Princeton, NJ: Princeton University Press, 1983), 376.

¹⁹Ibid., 377.

²⁰ Paulo Freire, *Pedagogy of the Oppressed*, trans. Myra Ramos (New York: Herder and Herder, 1970), 120–121.

²¹ Edward F. Edinger, *An American Jungian: Edward F. Edinger in Conversation with Lawrence Jaffe*, videocassette [3 tapes]. Produced and directed by Dianne D. Cordic (Los Angeles: 1990).

²² Parker Palmer, *The Courage to Teach: Exploring the Inner Landscape of the Teacher's Life* (San Francisco: Jossey-Bass, 1998), 4.

²³ Ibid., 4–5.

²⁴ Ibid., 11.

²⁵ Sri Sathya Sai Baba, The Educare Institute (2003–2007). *Educare Method Defined by Sri Sathya Sai Baba*, http://www.educare.org (accessed July 28, 2007).

²⁶ J. Krishnamurti, "Educating the Educator: Abandoning Idealism in Teaching,"*Parabola: Myth, Tradition and the Search for Meaning* 25, no. 3 (2000): 85–89. .

²⁷ Ibid., 87.

²⁸ Katie Cannon, *Katie's Canon: Womanism and the Soul of the Black Community* (New York: Continuum International Publishing Group, 1995).

²⁹ Ibid., 141.

³⁰ C. F. Reynolds and J. Piirto Reynolds, "Depth Psychology and Giftedness: Bringing Soul to the Field of Talent Development and Giftedness," *Roeper Review* 27, no. 3

   (2005): 164–171.
31 Ibid., 166.
32 Ibid.
33 Ibid.
34 Marimba Ani, *Yurugu.*
35 Elizabeth J. Tisdell, *Exploring Spirituality and Culture in Adult and Higher Education* (San
   Francisco: Jossey-Bass, 2003).

36 Clifford Mayes, *Jung and Education: Elements of an Archetypal Pedagogy* (Lanham, MD:
   Rowman & Littlefield Education, 2005).
37 Oliver, "The Journey," *Dream Work,* 35.
38 Anne Lamott, *Plan B: Further Thoughts on Faith* (New York: Riverhead Books, 2005), 76.

"TRYING TO TOUCH WHAT MATTERS": CONFESSIONS OF A HIGH SCHOOL DROPOUT

Jennifer Leigh Selig

> *I know this appetite*
> *the greed of a poet*
> *or an empty woman*
> *trying to touch*
> *what matters.*
> ~Audre Lorde

Dear Ms. Selig,

Thank you so much for all the help you have given me with my writting skills. Even though I can't spell there nothing you could do for me there. I've enjoied my three years of having you as a teacher. You are very good at what you do. I also believed that you've helped people come to realized how different, but the same we really are. Thank you again for everything. I hope your up coming classes will give you more joy, than pain.
> *Thanks,*
> *Russell*

I have a keepsake box in my office at home. The box is full, brimming over with hundreds of letters, notes, and cards from students I taught over the sixteen years of my career as a high school teacher. Each student wrote to me because together we touched something that mattered. I have saved the letters because they matter to me. They fill me up, they leave me full-filled, they remind me of how fulfilling those sixteen years were. I loved (nearly) every minute in every period in every day in every week in every year I was there. If you were to open the box and read any one of those letters, you'd understand why.

Yet, I put in only sixteen years, and then, at the age of forty, I quit. When people ask me why I left, I have a pithy anecdote I often tell. I am teaching Freshman English again for the first time in years. A boy struts into my classroom and proclaims in front of everyone that I taught his mother. I laugh out loud. "I've only been teaching for fifteen years," I tell him. "My mom was sixteen when she had me," he replies snidely. He was an ass all year long. She was pregnant when she was in my class, and she gave birth to this ass who then tortured me fifteen years later in the same classroom. It was time to leave.

But that's not the truth. The truth is, I became a casualty of the standardized test and its by-product, a bastardized education. I am the teacher "No Child Left Behind" left behind. I am a high school dropout. And like many dropouts, though I have moved forward, I still look back with regret.

Regret? REGRET? You feel regret that you left public "lower" education and secured a better paying job in private "upper" education? Isn't this the American dream: upward mobility?

The same people who would raise this question with incredulity are the very ones who used to ask me another question: "What do you do for a living?" When I told them I taught high school, they would lower their eyes along with their voices and say, "Ohhhh. That must be so hard," in a commiserating tone, as if I had just told them I worked in a prison guarding the worst of the worst offenders. In part, I filled the box for them. I imagined overturning it, watching those hundreds of letters, notes, and cards flutter and fall like so many flower petals at their feet.

I'd reply, "You should be so blessed."

~   ~   ~

"You will be so blessed," I tell the teacher candidates who take my Curriculum Development class at Mount St. Mary's College on our first day together. I share the oft-quoted Lee Iacocca sentence, "In a completely rational society, the best of us would be teachers and the rest of us would have to settle for something else." Then I ask them to share with the class something about their favorite teacher, the one who inspired them to enter the profession. After they introduce their teachers, I ask them to tell us why that teacher was so influential. I listen carefully to the stories. Sometimes it's, "She made me feel special." At other times it's, "She saw me." "He cared about me." "He encouraged me during a time when it was really hard for me." "When my dad died, she came to the funeral." Never is it, "She really helped prepare me for the standardized test." Never, "He stayed so close to the state standards." It's never the standardization students appreciate but the individualization. "She made *me* feel special." "He gave *me* a book he knew *I* would love." "He recognized *my* ability to draw, and encouraged *me*."

Even those who recognize their teacher's infectious love for the subject matter often remember little of that subject matter itself. For instance, one young woman remembered a physics teacher who would dress up like a mad scientist on lab days, but when I asked her to describe the content of the labs, she couldn't remember any of them. Another remembered his teacher's love for poetry but could only recall one of the poems she had loved. Some remembered disliking the subject matter themselves and marveling that someone else could love it so.

What mattered in the educational encounter? I asked. What did these stories have in common? On the chalkboard, we note the similarities: it's the human connection, the passion, the eros, the joy of learning, the journey from having a question to finding an answer. It's seldom the answer itself.

But education these days is obsessed with the answer. The outcome. The measurable learning result. Objectives, not subjectives like passion, like attention, like encouragement, like love. We have forgotten Einstein's *other* theory of relativity: "Not everything that can be counted counts, and not everything that counts can be counted." In education today, it's all about what can be counted, measured, assessed, quantified.

Ultimately, I quit teaching high school because I did not want to teach (only) what can be counted. I wanted to be un-accountable. This didn't mean I wanted to leave students behind, but rather it meant that I simply couldn't see students as mere accounts received. They were beautiful, unique, individual souls, and I did not want to see them standardized. I wanted them all to take something different from my classes, something that mattered to them, in the same way that I wanted to bring something different to my classes, something that mattered to me.

Dear Ms. Selig,

I especially want to thank you for being my teacher. No where have I learned as much as I did in your class and in your presence and what I appreciate most about this knowledge is the way you teach it. Rather than throwing facts and truths at us, you give us ideas to evaluate for ourselves. The things you teach are empowering and give us more freedom. W don't have to believe them, we don't have to like them, but the fact that we experienced them gives another dimension to our lives and a lucidity to look at the world, through enlightened eyes, if only for a moment but possibly forever.

Love,
Lisa

~ ~ ~

I began my career in my twenties as an English teacher. I fantasized about inviting great works of literature into the classroom and delving into them in a way that would deepen and ripen and transfigure us all. Literature was not an object to learn but a subject to learn from, the venue for touching what mattered. For me, it wasn't *Romeo and Juliet* that mattered, it was love that mattered, and *Romeo and Juliet* gave us the excuse to discuss love in the classroom.

The teachers in my department taught *Romeo and Juliet* according to their passions and gifts, emphasizing different parts of the plot, different themes, using different strategies to make Shakespeare's language and story come alive. Mr. Clark was also the drama teacher, so he had students up in front of the room acting out the play, staging mock fights with construction paper swords, directing Juliet onto a desk for the balcony scene, handing Romeo a Diet Coke to use as poison in the death scene. Mrs. Reed was our teacher with the greatest sense of humor, so she painstakingly deconstructed all the obscure and bawdy puns until the students were falling out of their seats in hysterics. Ms. Barker was a purist about the classics, and she would read aloud the most lyrical passages, her eyes filling, then spilling over with tears. Students in all of our classes got a different experience of Shakespeare—from an appreciation of his staging to his sense of humor, from the beauty of his language to the universality of his expression of youthful love—each experience intimately tied to the passion of the teacher.

Some will disagree, but it seems right to me to teach in this way. There is no one Shakespeare, and there is no one response to Shakespeare. What mattered was not that students all received the same Shakespeare but that they had a passionate encounter with Shakespeare facilitated by a passionate teacher.

However, standardization changed all that. First, we were told by the head of Curriculum Development for the district that we must have students write an essay as the final assessment. Gone were Mr. Clark's videotaped performances shown at Back to School Night; gone were Mrs. Reed's "one-pun-upmanship" competitions in which students wrote their own Shakespearean puns; gone were Ms. Barker's Globe Theatre Days for which students memorized and delivered a soliloquy in costume, all gone because they took too much time away from writing the essay. Gone too was my particular essay topic comparing teenage love in the 16th century with today, because that wasn't deemed *what mattered most* for students to take away from the play.

Of course, I am being extreme here. No matter how standardized the final assessment on *Romeo and Juliet*, no one can stop a teacher from talking about the theme of love in the play. No one can stop a teacher from staging a scene, from deconstructing a pun, from waxing eloquent on the lyricism of the language. It wasn't that those things were squeezed out entirely; it's just that we had to fight for time to squeeze them in. It *felt* extreme, as the classroom increasingly became a battleground where we each had to fight to teach what we felt extremely important.

I became greedy over time. "Hurry up and learn this stuff so we can talk about the good stuff," I'd tell my students.

Ms. Selig,

I just wanted you to know that I have a lot of respect for you as a teacher and I admire you as a person. You are one of the only teachers that makes me feel like the stuff I'm doing is going to help me somehow and usually you tell us straight up if it's not all that important. You are the absolute no nonsense teacher. What an honest thing. I love it that you tell it like it is. I find it so great that you leave in your personality while you teach. That's the kind of thing that makes a student trust a teacher and it's very important to me.

Sincerely,
Mario

As heart and soul and spirit were squeezed out of the English curriculum, I felt the heart and soul and spirit squeezed out of me. Though Mario felt I left in my personality while I taught, my personality felt caught in an ethical trap. On the one hand, I had to "teach to the test" because the test was tied to students' grades, and their grades were tied to their futures; I couldn't ruin their chances of getting into the college of their dreams because I didn't prepare them for the test. On the other hand, the curriculum felt empty to me, and I felt the hunger, the appetite, the "greed of a poet" raging within me as it raged within them as well.

After a decade of vocational bliss, I considered quitting the teaching profession. I struggled, wrestled, grappled, resisted, thrashed about in my own turmoil. I wanted to stay. I looked for compromise. If the soul was being squeezed out of the English curriculum, I thought, then I'd introduce it somewhere else. I proposed teaching mythology as a semester-long elective course. It was accepted. I taught mythology as ancient psychology, following the philosophy of Joseph Campbell. I organized the course around "the big questions"—Where did we come from? What happens to us when we die? What makes life worth living? What is worth dying for? What is the relationship between humanity and divinity? What is love?

The class was so popular that we added a second section, and the next year a second semester. Scads of the letters, notes, and cards in my keepsake box are from students who took those classes.

Dear Ms. Selig,

A lot of what you said is true, how mythology ties everything together. And I did get a lot out of this course. I would like to study psychology in terms

74

of mythological concepts, that totally intrigued me. It has opened up my mind to much more new information that I can take in and apply to myself or others. It's funny how I kept on thinking through the love unit, that if people studied mythology and psychology and understood the stages of love, there wouldn't be so many problems among people. I do feel I have died and become someone new.

Love,

Vanessa

I felt like I died and ascended to heaven after reading that letter. Mythology was the Holy Grail, that grand adventure that led us deep into the heart of the questions that matter the most. Though I still taught English, I lived for the periods in which I taught mythology.

That period was short-lived.

After several years of ever-increasing popularity, the class was canceled, along with many other electives. "More college-prep courses" was the cry. "Back to basics," it was decreed. It's not that the course doesn't matter, my principal explained to me. It's just that it doesn't count.

I'm not arguing here against teaching the basics. Nouns matter. Love is a noun, and it matters. Love is also a verb. When I change it to *loving*, it becomes a gerund. Gerunds might be on the test, but whether you love, what you love, why you love whom you love, how loving you are—*what really matters*—will not be tested. This is good— love should not be tested. But it should be taught. Not taught as in "Let's tell students *what to think* about love," but taught as in "Let's teach students *to think* about love and give them a place to explore *what others think* about love, so they can refine *what they think* about love." Riffing off Einstein's quote above, there is a difference between what should be taught and what should be tested. Not everything testable should be taught. Not everything taught can be or should be tested.

I felt like *I* was being tested, my principles against my principal's decision. After teaching mythology, I was convinced more than ever that students were hungry for a meaning-full curriculum. I proposed a psychology class and made sure that it met the requirements (that it counted) for a college-prep course. It was accepted. I taught it for several years. It was the best thing I ever taught. Still more letters, notes, and cards in my keepsake box are from students in those classes.

Several are from students' mothers; one of them stands out like no other.

Amber was an exceptional student in my psychology class during her senior year. A week before graduation, I received a letter from her mother. I had just published a gift book for graduates, and she bought a copy and wanted me to sign it as a gift for Amber. The letter read, in part:

> *I would also like to take this opportunity to thank you for the admirable job you have done with her psychology class this semester. I recognized the enthusiasm you must exude by Amber's behavior and comments right away. She has continued throughout this semester to discuss what she has heard and learned in class. The thought-provoking topics also gave our family opportunities to share with each other ideas we might not have shared otherwise. Amber has expressed the desire to "tread the waters" of psychology in college, and possibly as a career choice. Your class has helped Amber realize that she has empathy with other people and a strong desire to learn more about them. With your encouragement and enthusiasm, she is showing more passion about her future.*

Two weeks later, Amber was dead, killed in a car accident. I took it hard. I cared for her. But I took some small measure of solace that before her death, she was closer to her mother than ever. Though she had no future, in the last months of her life she and her mother shared a more meaningful present. They touched what mattered, and the psychology curriculum had played a part in that, had served as a bridge between mother and daughter where together they could stand with more open hearts and minds.

Two years later, the standardization ax fell on the psychology class, and it was canceled too. I lost heart. I stayed one more year until the boy strutted into my class and told me in front of everyone that I had taught his mother. I quit. I walked away with a box full of letters, notes, and cards. I walked in circles for a year. I couldn't return, but I couldn't stay away. Eventually I found my way into higher education.

~   ~   ~

My first university course was one in an education department where I taught curriculum design. Instead of teaching the standards to secondary students, I was now teaching future teachers how to teach the standards to secondary students. *The more things change, the more they stay the same.* I still left my personality in. "I'll teach you the stages of curriculum design," I told the students, "but the techniques and tools and strategies in the book are not what matters. The heart and soul of teaching begins in the heart and soul of the teacher. So tell us about your favorite teacher, the one who inspired you to be here today."

They tell stories about those teachers, amazing teachers, unique teachers, no two teachers the same. And then I say, "You were in their class for 180 days, 180 hours. Tell me what you did in those hours."

They can't account for them. "He made me think," one student shares about a beloved history teacher.

"About what?" I reply. "What was the curriculum? What did you do in all those hours?"

She furls her brow. "I don't remember, I just remember he made me think so hard sometimes I'd leave class with a headache." We smile. We all recognize good teaching, though we have no idea what the goods were he was teaching.

These are not students who are decades away from high school themselves. These are students in their early twenties being asked to recall what happened five, six, seven years ago. And so I ask: "If you've already forgotten the vast majority of the curriculum you learned from your favorite teacher, what are the implications for your own teaching, for your own curriculum development?"

The room is silent. We sit steeped in the question, which is really a koan. I can hear their minds racing, their hearts beating, their stomachs growling. They are hungry poets too, every one of them. We all know one thing—that we want to teach because we believe it matters. Soon, someone raises the question, "But how can I teach what I believe matters if I have to cover all this material for the standardized state exams?"

Everyone looks at me. I look out the window. There is no easy answer to this in sight. I turn them instead to look at a myth, to the moment in the search for the Holy Grail where Percival learns to ask, "Whom does the Grail serve?" Together we wonder over the question, "Whom does education serve?" Students, society, state . . . whom does education serve? Whom do we as teachers serve?

Perhaps I am not the best one to guide them through the rough and tumble of these thorny questions and koans. After all, I am the teacher "No Child Left Behind" left behind. I am a high school dropout. I am full of regret, not only personal regret but public regret that this is the state of education these students who strive to become teachers inherit today. I share with them my questions, my struggles, my successes and failures, my strategies for resistance, my regrets, all of which are mine but not mine alone. They are shared by many teachers: those who had the courage of their convictions and dropped out, and those who have the courage of their convictions and stay in. I am not the first who stayed and asked, "Should I leave?" I am not the last to leave and ask, "Should I have stayed?" I am not the only one out who asks, "Should I go back in?" And then, "Could I go back in?"

Today, I tell them, we must be content with questions with no easy answers. In the meantime, I have returned from my journey toward the Holy Grail with gifts. I overturn the keepsake box. Hundreds of letters, notes, and cards flutter and fall like so many flower petals at our feet. At the end of the day, I tell those future teachers, may you be left holding a box full of letters, notes, and cards, each one saying

> *Dear Teacher,*
> *You taught me, and it mattered.*
> *Love,*
> *Your Student*

We should all be so blessed.

SOUL-CENTERED EDUCATION: AN INTERVIEW WITH STEPHEN AIZENSTAT

Nancy Treadway Galindo

NANCY: Almost certainly, all of us appreciate the importance of education and share a common aspiration to nourish and improve education in today's world. In this context, would you share your advocacy for "teaching with soul," and would you describe this quality of teaching in the classroom?

STEVE: In my experience, teaching in a soul-centered way engages imagination and elicits story. When you bring story into the classroom, the subject matter and information become animated. You can tell a story about anything. Teaching history is a great example because story will bring history to life as a living actuality. Story takes students into a historical moment in imagination and allows them to explore it in a three-dimensional way. On the contrary, History is most often taught as a chronology of wars, dates, and events. What's vital to remember is that each moment in history is filled with personal stories and experiences and the extent to which the teacher incorporates these stories is the extent to which the students can deepen into their own stories and life experiences.

There truly is a difference between teaching in a soul-centered way and teaching that fundamentally conveys information. In the latter, the teacher is little more than a delivery system. So often, when I was teaching junior and senior high school, I was asked to train young people in the mastery of information. The curriculum was generally predetermined and we were required to test and assess students based on prescribed chapter units. Frankly, I often felt as if I was a functionary communicating programmed data. There was a built-in routine with the textbook as well. Students would read a chapter, after which we would complete the chapter review, take the practice test, correct it, then take the final test, and finally proceed to the next chapter. In English, History and Geography, the subjects I taught, that kind of teaching really missed what I would call a soul-centered approach.

NANCY: How do you recognize a classroom that's "soul-centered" from one that's not?

STEVE: If you imagine two History classrooms, in the first classroom, the teacher is truly doing a great job, imparting information and offering narrative. He or she is talking about what happened, giving dates and events, naming notable people, and describing the wars and crises that were going on at the time.

Offering narrative is quite different than telling story. Narrative is an account of what happened, whereas story is multi-dimensional. Story is animated with multi-faceted experiences. It's engaging, surprising, and unpredictable. To know a period of history is to know an array of stories and experiences that bring the historical facts and chronologies to life.

If you imagine the second classroom, the teacher is describing the same period of history and telling a story about an individual who was living at the time. The story brings the individual's felt presence into the room. The teacher is describing how the individual is dressed, what he or she is doing, reading, thinking about, or struggling with. The teacher is engaging the student's imagination and experience, and therefore, engaging the soul. This teacher, in contrast to the first one, is offering a soul-centered approach to teaching and learning.

NANCY: When you're in the classroom, what do you look for that shows you that students are engaged in a soul-centered way?

STEVE: I think it's helpful to contrast students' engagement in a soulless classroom, and in a soul-centered classroom. In a soulless classroom, students generally sit in straight rows of chairs. They're looking up at the teacher, and for the most part they're listening to the lesson and jotting down the facts and figures they need to memorize for the exam. It's routine. The students know they're going to be evaluated, so the information is filtered through their rational minds for the purpose of doing well on the test. In a soulless classroom, many students are preoccupied in imagination while the teacher is routinely reciting information.

In a soul-centered classroom, there's something else going on. Students are so interested and involved in the subject matter that the test is the last thing they're thinking about. They're captivated by imagination, participating in the activity of the classroom, experiencing the material, and appreciating how the material affects them. What's going on in the classroom invites their involvement and excitement. The students are fully engaged in their participation. It's truly a lived-experience wherein a sense of presence informs the material in dialogue with the students.

NANCY: It sounds like a dynamic and animating experience for the students. Would you say so?

STEVE: Yes, a soul-centered classroom is a lively classroom. Everyone brings his or her life experience into conversation with one another. It's a dialogical experience. It's not about churning out information. The classroom revolves around the students' experiences as well as their ability to share and interact with one another. It's quite a remarkably different experience for them than just absorbing the facts in order to pass the test.

In a soul-centered classroom, there are also lots of things to look at. The teacher will bring in pictures and put them up on the walls. Whether the subject is Literature, History, or Math, students can look around the room and see equations, important people, and engaging illustrations of events. The moment the students walk into a soul-centered classroom, they're walking into a realm of stimulation, imagination, new discovery, excitement, and engagement. Their senses are touched and activated, and their life experience is evoked and appreciated.

NANCY: I know teachers are interested in how to elicit this sort of stimulation and inspiration. What would you offer from your experience?

STEVE: When I teach, the first thing I do is rediscover what excites me about the subject. This is the beginning of a soul-centered approach. It isn't nearly enough though. The next question is: what in my actual lived-experience is stimulated now, and what fascinates me about the subject? I need to engage my curiosity about the material and keep it alive. Activating my own interest and fascination is the key that opens the door to a soul-centered classroom. I might be fascinated by how the topic is relevant to current events or what can be made of the material from multiple perspectives. When I become curious about the subject and follow that curiosity, it takes me beyond the textbook and into story, poetry, biography, and into contemporary magazines, newspapers, videos, and films.

Once I start getting curious, I invite the curiosity and fascination of the kids. Then they're going to discover things and put things together that couldn't otherwise be imagined. This is the key. This is what makes the difference between good soul-centered teaching and extraordinary soul-centered teaching.

NANCY: This shift from good teaching to extraordinary teaching is important. Would you describe some of the ways you do this?

STEVE: I design activities that allow the kids to explore the curriculum in creative ways that aren't already programmed and predetermined. Doing so invites what's surprising and unpredictable to present itself. It enlivens the content and cultivates creativity and invention. Creativity and invention aren't oppositional to planned content. Planned content will provide the important foundation and skeletal structure, whereas creativity and invention moves students into critical thinking and methods of analysis that are extraordinarily useful and constructive. When students get the creative juices flowing, and get inventive, they will access the part of their intelligence that makes memorization and the tracking of the planned content and chronology much easier and certainly more relevant.

NANCY: In a soul-centered classroom, what generates fascination and curiosity?

STEVE: First and foremost, there's a teacher who's not a tyrant, enforcing order and silence—nor is that teacher a pushover, permitting distraction and chaos. Rather the teacher is someone who lives in his or her artistry and mastery of the material, and in sheer enjoyment of the art of teaching and evoking the student's organic interest in the material. The teacher is lively, active, and curious.

Secondly, in a soul-centered classroom, kids are talking with one another. They're engaged in conversation about what they're studying. They might be taking up a topic in groups of two, four, or six. They might be having a debate or getting ready to have a competition about the subject with another group of students. Kids are working together with other kids, evoking each other's interest and learning in a peer-oriented way. There's talking back and forth yet its not chaotic or without purpose. The conversation is interactive and relevant, not only to the material, but also to how the material lives in the students' experiences and in their lives. Remarkable surprises happen when everyone is engaged in the material in this way.

Furthermore, a soul-centered classroom isn't confining or sterile like a factory or assembly line, with rows of students whose sole purpose is to master and memorize the information that's required to pass the exam. On the contrary, the room itself is alive with images on the walls, and it's animated with the vibration of the kids' interest. The chairs are arranged so that they encourage conversation. When students enter the room, they feel engaged, their eyes are opened, their senses are stimulated, and they're in a community of conversation. Both the teacher and the students are in an interactive learning community with one another. It's an engaging community.

NANCY: When you're in this environment of curiosity, conversation, and community, what happens for you as the teacher?

STEVE: I'm satisfied—and I feel fulfilled. When the students and I have collectively engaged the material, I know I've helped them move along with their own creative learning process.

I also get enormous satisfaction from utilizing multiple learning styles so all the students have the opportunity to grow, develop, and shine. To watch a child's eyes, a young person's eyes, or an adult's eyes light up because they've rediscovered the joy of learning, is probably one of the most fulfilling experiences I know in my life as an educator.

This happens in a soul-centered classroom when multiple learning opportunities are made available to students.

NANCY: Given students' different learning styles, how do you evaluate their work?

STEVE: When the time comes I use a multiple set of evaluation tools. We have an exam because I believe that knowing the material is important, but I use additional methods of evaluation as well. There are only 20 to 30 percent of the kids in any classroom that are good at memorizing facts and figures and answering multiple-choice questions. These 20 to 30 percent of the students fit right into the assessment methodology that's currently utilized in virtually 100 percent of the public schools. This assessment methodology is based on the necessary funding for "No Child Left Behind."

Nevertheless, there are additional learning styles that I attend to when I'm making assessments. Some kids excel at creative writing, poetry, and theatric production. Other kids learn best in a group of other students where they can interact, imagine, and invent ways of understanding the material and how it applies to their lives and their community. Others excel at computer design and production, and they are technologically gifted. Some kids are so articulate that if you put them in front of the class and let them go, they'll shine.

On the contrary, if you ask them to write, they'll have the most difficult time with spelling and grammar. Many kids are either dyslexic or have some kind of ADHD and have the hardest time even filling in the little bubbles on the answer forms for the test. Yet, if they're encouraged to be creative, expressive, and expansive in the classroom, they can come forward with ideas that are just spectacular and off the page. They can think creatively and holistically, and go beyond familiar formulations. A soul-centered perspective encourages this use of a range of assessment methodologies that will encourage individual abilities and talents.

NANCY: Would you say more about how to cultivate creativity and imagination, and how to tend to the heart and soul of the student?

STEVE: Carl Jung said that creativity is one of our instincts, yet so often, we forget to encourage it and include it. When we do, we can cultivate the creative impulse and listen to imagination as it expresses itself through gesture, dream, and vision. This is vital because it helps us become more of who we are and allows us to connect back to the authenticity that lives within us. Creativity is what supports and fuels our capacity to think and act more effectively.

Little kids are always engaged in creative and imaginative play of one sort or the next. They bop about in nature. They play with invisible playmates. Parents and older people appear bigger than life and they're imbued with strengths and powers of giant figures in epic stories. Kids learn more in those first three or four years than they learn in decades of education. How do they do that? Are they reading books? No. Are they modeling and mimicking? Yes, of course. Are they in imaginative play? Yes. It seems to me then, that it's critically important to cultivate imagination, not lose it, not push it out as something that's alien to the educative process, but rather to value it front and center. Creativity and imaginative play support our psychic life, our passions, libido, and good health. Moreover, creativity and imagination stimulate and support our rational thinking and analytical capabilities.

When I consider how to "educate" the heart, mind, and soul of the student, I bear in mind that the soul is the realm that lives between the heart and emotions. It embraces aesthetic and imaginative ways of experiencing. The mind traditionally includes the realm of rational thinking, developmental thinking, analytical skills, and the capacity to utilize mathematical calculations, scientific methodologies, and the causal relationship of things. The cultivation of the mind, along with the cultivation of the emotional and aesthetic life, are both profoundly important. The soul bridges both and offers something to both. Moreover, the soul is the intelligence that lives at the center of both. From a soul-centered perspective, I recognize the importance of thinking imaginatively. I know that when students are in touch with their visions, reveries, and dreams, they're living their lives sourced by the imaginative spring. This is the primary ground.

NANCY: It seems evident that your approach to soul-centered teaching extends beyond the classroom. Would you talk about this?

STEVE: Well, I think this goes to the purpose of education in today's world. Clearly it's important for the evolution of our species and the planet that we are the best we can be intellectually, emotionally, and spiritually. When we support the imaginative process in the classroom, it opens students to multiple perspectives. This is so important because we're citizens of a global community as well as a local community. In addition to having our particular identities that are connected to our family, our country, or our ethnic tribe, we are also interrelated to everything and everybody around us, to the creatures, forests, and ecosystems, as well as to the multiple cultures that exist throughout the world. Today, we're so closely connected to diverse cultures by air travel and technology. We can appreciate that what's going on halfway around the world has a direct impact on our own lives because it's the very thing we're using, wearing, or eating at the moment. We're closely connected in all of these ways.

In the global community, we're being asked to embrace multiple perspectives. We need to understand what it's like to be in the experience of others around the world. When we're in the realm of imagination, we're open to multiple points of view by definition. Imagination embraces things poetically. I believe it's the request, the challenge, and really the plea of the planet, for teachers to open up to imagination, and open up to multiple perspectives so that our students can move into a more deeply felt sense of empathetic regard for everyone and everything around us. It's quite critical at the moment.

The other important concept for teachers to address is paradox. So many things are no longer yes or no, right or wrong, or black or white. Circumstances in the world are complex and complicated. There isn't one right way or one right answer. What's true today may be false tomorrow. In fact, things are both true and false at the same time. Consequently, it's important to teach the capacity to hold paradox.

In addition, kids need to learn how to learn. Some of them will change professions five or ten times in their lifetimes and learning to learn will support them with these changes. Others will hold on to the same profession for 20, 30, or 40 years. In any case, everyone's skill-sets need to include the ability to deal with change and paradox.

NANCY: As the president of a graduate institute, you interface with the marketplace and with prospective employers. What have you learned about their satisfaction or their expectation of the educational establishment?

STEVE: I became sharply aware of this recently, when I was invited to a seminar that was given by our regional accrediting agency. Each year the presidents of the universities and colleges in our region come together to discuss the state of education and dialogue about the issues that concern us.

At this particular gathering, the accrediting agency invited five CEOs from some of our most prestigious multi-national corporations. They were asked to offer their perspectives on education in today's world, particularly for the high school, college, and university levels. In turn, the CEOs asked something of us. What they asked was surprising and alarming, and at the same time, it made darn good sense. To the shock of most of us, they asked us not to narrow the focus of education, nor confine students to a sharply focused pedagogy or curriculum. They offered that what's now being required in the global marketplace is innovation, experimentation, the facility to grasp complex problems, and the ability to come up with new, untried, and never-before imagined solutions. The old methods aren't working, they told us. Their plea was for us to keep imagination and creative thinking alive and vibrant in our schools, colleges, and universities.

The second thing they asked of us was not to train students into a particular vocation. This shocked everyone in the room. Their rationale was that once students come out of our colleges and universities, they can train them in the necessary corporate skill-sets within three to six months, and do it in a much more effective way than we can. They assured us that the necessary skill-sets are going to change in four years anyway, and they're in the best possible position to track and train for these. What they said they can't do, and they asked us to do in an extraordinary way, is give students a firm, rooted grounding in the liberal arts and humanities.

In addition, they asked us to support our students in staying in relationship with their family, friends, and colleagues and to support them in developing a rich and meaningful inner and outer life. They emphasized that this was far more important than any skill-building we could do. They offered that the people in their companies who are educated in the humanities and liberal arts are happier and more fulfilled as human beings. They observed that these people are more deeply in touch with their humanity and their humility. They stressed that these are the kind of people they value and seek. They pointed out that these folks are innovative, creative, and have a satisfying sense of their own experience and personhood. They told us that their experience confirms that these people stay with the company and help everyone move forward. They pointed out, to the contrary, that people who are narrowly focused don't do well. These people don't think off the chart, and they have the hardest time with their own satisfaction with life, and with their jobs. They get depressed and go through all sorts of problems, emotionally, psychologically, and physiologically. Furthermore, their family dynamics don't work very well.

The corporate executives brought home to us that a narrow, specialized education isn't what they're looking for. What they're looking for is a return to a renaissance education rooted in the humanities and liberal arts. Even when we're teaching coursework in science, physics, chemistry, engineering, and other new fields, they asked us to root our teaching in the humanities and liberal arts. In the meeting, you could hear a pin drop. It was astonishing, and afterwards, the educators looked at one another and agreed that it made enormously good sense. These executives knew something that we didn't.

NANCY: It's striking how this ties back into what you were saying about inviting soul, imagination, and fascination into the classroom.

STEVE: Yes. That's what the heads of these multi-national corporations were asking us to do: keep curiosity, imagination, and fascination alive in the classroom and in our students. They asked us to encourage our students' sense of wonderment and inspiration. They asked us to urge them to reach beyond the ordinary to what's extraordinary—and entirely possible—in their lives, and in the world. They asked us to nourish their sense of humanity and encourage them to be involved and engaged in diverse relationships. They implored us not to close them down. They urged us to allow them to open up and love them. If we would send these sorts of students to them, they assured us that they could give them the required skill-sets easily enough. What they couldn't do, they told us, was incubate and cultivate their sense of wonderment and imagination that opens from the inside out. The entire conversation with these multi-national corporate executives was a confirmation of our call for soul-centered teaching.

WHAT WHITE WHALE BREACHES?
CLASSROOM AS SACRED SPACE

Dennis Patrick Slattery

But Truth is the silliest thing under the sun.
Try to get a living by the Truth—and go to the Soup Societies. Heavens!

Once, not too many years ago, during a break in a course on Dante's *Commedia*, one of my students approached me to convey with warming enthusiasm and bewilderment the following insight: "I read Dante's poem and know full well that I understand little of it, but I understand so much of my own life having read and then discussed it in class." An interesting angle she exposed to me about reading poetry, and this poem specifically: whether one grasps a great deal or a few valued chips of the work's bigger block, it still has the capacity to change or alter perception, to widen the orbit of what one grasps of self and world in some new conjunctive constellations.

In the classroom, a work of fiction or non-fiction for that matter, if brought in as a guest to the course's setting, has the capacity to unleash its energy into the collective psyche of the members in the room, to be amplified, or like a beam through a magnifying glass, to gather the power to start a fire, to kindle something deep in the woody pulp of the soul, to fire it up, to create a reservoir of *enthusiasmos*, a word used to convey the presence of "a god within," often in the figure of Dionysos, such that learning occurs on a more advanced and vertical level and thereby gains the capacity to alter a human being. Sometimes all one need do is notice innuendo, which can by itself be sufficient spark to ignite a forest fire.

The essay that follows is therefore more experiential than scholarly in the sense that it will not be preoccupied with mustering and mastering evidence from primary and secondary sources for either support or persuasive mucilage. Rather, I wish to muse in memory for a few moments on what my experience of a good classroom experience consists of, what I have watched occur and what conditions often coagulate to attend such a pole of pedagogy. The consequences of such a class are nothing short of miraculous; time and space themselves alter to accommodate and actually participate in the conversion through conversation. Converse is the Appian Way to such a change of heart.

I have in recent years been both further amazed and more curious about how, for example, in teaching Herman Melville's classic whale tale, *Moby-Dick,* that in the 25 years of boarding the Pequod and signing on yet one more time, always with a new crew, I have noticed that the same white whale has never breached in the classroom twice in just the same fluky way. Yes, the text is the same, and, no, it is not. True enough, the words tattooed on the pages are fixed "with firmest fortitude." But the similarities of these two deliveries ends right there: one might as well use a map to describe to another who has not ventured forth, the experiences one has had in journeying across the far field. What happens in the elixir of the classroom that accounts for such a phenomenon? I suspect, without wanting to develop here this corridor of thought, that an alchemical mixture of myths and imaginations that comprise the particular group of students in the room has everything to do with the differences that emerge in this same poem.

It seems then that there are three clusters of authority that arise in the classroom: the poem itself, the teacher, and the voices of the individual students. The fourth cluster, if it can be addressed right here, is what the three groups together create in the admixture of myth, memory, and meaning that constitutes the emergence of wisdom when these varied and yet united forces of psychic energy coalesce in a common conversation. Sensing and nurturing this soulful engagement is worth all the effort it requires. Sustaining it, however, is a difficult and diffident matter. A few assumptions are active in this process as well. Here is my short list, always with an impulse to grow longer at a moment's notice:

1. The text is not an object to be analyzed and squeezed but an organic subject that changes and accommodates, to a large degree, the changes in the reader. The story is another member of the class, one who has paid its tuition to the registrar of history and to the lively tradition formed within it. The students comprise in part the narratives that engage this central meta-text.

2. Submission to the work and to the voices in the room changes the barometric pressure gathering and gleaming in the pages of the narrative.

3. The poem harbors its own autonomy—even its own mythos—but is more than willing to oblige the particular congregation of people who gather around it, not unlike how tribal members gather around a communal fire, to be illuminated and even warmed by an ancient tribal narrative. The poem is the communal fire of the course, whatever course the discussion may take within its grooved catalogue description.

4. Stories have a sacred and numinous quality that cannot ever be completely rendered, but it can be experienced, not once but often, even felt viscerally and responded to with largesse and by means of tentative assertions that may shift in emphasis or degree at any point, depending on how faithful one wishes to be to the narrative design, the warp and woof of the story.

5. One should be willing to be guided by the work rather than attempt mastery of it, or to colonize it to fit a prescribed idea, or even rape it—yes, I have heard that language in an NEH Seminar one year—or to treat it as a dead object, to be discarded, subsequently, as a dried husk or a rind, deprived of its nourishing gnosis.

6. Reading a text is not done for information but for some deeper, more imaginal and subtler level and authority of transformation through insight reached mutually in the shared conversion of reader, text and classroom interchange.

7. Relinquishing some key components of one's own authority, prejudices, narrowness, ideological huffing and puffing, allows the work greater expansion, to speak with greater amplitude and density and to be heard with more generous ears of the heart.

8. What one grasps from a work is tentative and good for that reading or discussion only; subsequent readings will yield further and often different and even contrary insights.

9. Deep in the core of a text is a living mythos that behaves like a smoldering nugget of the work's *raison de etre,* its existence and power. Each reading may take the reader closer on his/her pilgrimage to that hot center of meaning.
10. A work read silently in private is not the same text that enters the classroom; the collective wisdom, energy, gathering of just this set of mythologems changes, influences the work's trajectory, its disclosure, orbit and ultimate meaning, especially as the words pilgrimage from silence to sound to be heard by the collective ears of the class.
11. Rereading is a key imaginal re-engagement to understanding on a deeper level what one glimpsed only partially in earlier readings.
12. Reading passages aloud changes the dynamics and the atmosphere of the classroom as a *temenos.* The air changes, the energy shifts hither and yon, down and up, even as participants are transformed in the process of understanding as an experience. Understanding seems to me to contain its own form of human experience.
13. A field of energy is created in the room that is both fragile and ephemeral, yet durable in its own way, much as a morphic field of energy oscillates, dissipates, and intensifies during the experience of reading.
14. At stake in the conversation where an energy flow begins to be created between the work and the individual who participates within a collective, is language itself as the fundamental but not exclusive mediator of meaning. Language itself, then, is redeemed in the act of learning through and by means of a text. Psychic energy emanates from the turbines of language that comprise its creative power.

I am sure there are others to list, but these are sufficient for this round. Not dogmatic assertions that push the text off center stage that is then filled with the student's own narrative, the new bouquet on the dining room table of learning; rather, the insights gleaned, while moving through the mythology of the student, bends like the colored rays of a rainbow, back to the pot of gold of the text, from whence the original *enthusiasmos* emanates, like a flow of grace, and to where it ends.

I am interested as well in this delineation of the experience of a good class, as well as in the oral power of a text when it is read aloud by teacher and student. Some quality of the work gains amplitude and suggestive cache in existence by this process of oral reading such that what has been silent contributes in its sound to yet another level of the text's own consciousness. I would push this idea a bit further to assert that a level of *poiesis* is activated in the interchange of text, student and teacher wherein something new is created, made, shaped, contoured, adapted even, that transforms the body of people gathered around the fire of the text—and in the fire of the imagination that illumines all. I call this phenomenal experience *mythopoiesis*: the mythos of the students as well as that of the text are transformed in a shared transaction.

In an essay by James Hillman included in this volume, he develops the difference between civilization and culture. He presented these distinctions in the talk on which the essay is predicated, in 2005. However, almost 25 years earlier he offered an inaugural address to the Fellows of the newly-hatched Dallas Institute of Humanities and Culture, where he tracked the etymology of the word *culture*. I want to cite it here because of its affinities with classroom culture. His desire, as he states, is to promote with the word "a penumbra, a connotative atmosphere. It evoked 'cult'; it evoked the 'occult' (hard to see, deliberately hidden, esoteric, mystery) and 'culture' also evoked fermenting organic forms that grow in intense, warm, richly fed unnatural vessels."[2] In such a pedagogic Petri dish may a culture be organically formed, ripen, and then sprout new cultures, themselves to be nurtured to maturity.

Such a rich and organic image for the classroom cannot be surpassed. With the right temperature, the right care, the right nurturing and sustained vigilance, the imagination as cultural organ ripens into new insights, interpretations, and meanings. Such is the magic membrane of a classroom that nourishes the soul of knowledge.

Meaning, insight, and recognition are liquid qualities that stem from a sustained imaginal engagement with the archetypal realms of those verities that do not fade, die off, grow old and feeble, or crack open because of wear; rather, they are inflected in various ways in the moment of the event of just this kind of classroom experience. Less analysis than the powers of meditation and contemplation, reverie and musing move us closer to the soul's behaviors and love of perception. Reverie opens to an intersection, where the work's energy field has an opportunity, even an invitation, to work the force field of each participant. Knowledge and then insight are ends in themselves, not dependent therefore on career opportunities, promotions and raises.

Rather, they exist in the service of the enhancement of the life spirit, the soul life that allows one to deepen beyond the trivialities of what the world presents as important.

Years of teaching has claimed and supported the idea that the text loves conversation and its own participation in such social intercourse. It will, if given half an opportunity, speak back to what is addressed to it; it tends to speak differently on each rereading and response. The imaginal world that it invites conversation with is in truth more "real" than what is usually and unreflectively called "the real world" of job acquisition, traffic snarls and Dow Jones twitches. The culture indeed has it backward.

I believe this notion of the conversational quality of a text is important to pause on for another moment, for this reason: I had thought for many years that I was to engage a text as if it were complete in itself. I have come to realize the half-truth of such a premature assessment. I believe now that the text is both finished in itself and yet incomplete to its readers; the text, in fact, needs readers and conversations around it to gain an accretion of further emendations. By the same token, we who come to embrace its life blood, to argue with it, to become complicit with it, to rearrange it and ourselves in its structure, are also seeking a form of completion through the painful consciousness of our incompleteness. The text, in other words, completes something in me as I strive to add to its own completed, yet open, nature. Such is its own wily paradoxical structure of existence.

An extension of the above idea is that the text is self-conscious. Part of the excitement and crucial importance of the act of reading, then rereading and conversing with the text, is to expose that self-consciousness and our own self-reflective complicity in the process, indeed, the pilgrimage of reading. Added to this idea is one that implies the act of reading as another reenactment of the hero's journey: a departure from the normative world of convention and habit and worn-through ideas and assumptions each of us carries like unused valuables every day; entrance into the woods, if not the thick wilderness of the text, leaves one initially alone in one's own struggles in reading it; then an exit from that isolation to join in *communitas* to wrestle in a larger orbit with the forces of interpretation, with all of its misapprehensions. At this juncture, one carries from the woods of the work what one can claim as one's boon of insight, or knowledge, or a deeper grasping of the invisible reality that lurks and even lingers just below the water line of the words on the page. The page with its markings is the dark wood where one must heed the call and then enter it courageously in order to struggle with the forces that may retard or promote a deeper understanding.

Terza Rima as a Pattern of Learning

My sense recently is that such a struggle may be grasped most cogently in the structure that Dante Alighieri invented to carry the weight of his *Commedia*: the *terza rima* rhyme scheme. Such a structural scaffold in both architecture and content that accrues around it harbors the essential or primal pattern of psyche's motion in learning. Psyche is terza rimic; learning is the journey on this same pathway.

Let me give an example. In *Inferno* 1 Dante offers these three first lines:

> Nel mezzo del cammin di nostra vita (A)
> mi ritrovai per una selva oscura (B)
> che la dirrita via era smarrita (A)
> (When I had journeyed half of our life's way,
> I found myself within a shadowed forest,
> For I had lost the path that does not stray.)[3]

As I have assigned a letter for each of the last words in the line, we see that the first and third words rhyme. That is the *terza rima* rhyme scheme. However, we need one more *terza rima* in order to see its fuller progression:

> Ahi quanto a dir qual era e cosa dura (B)
> Esta selva selvaggia e aspra e forte (C)
> Che nel pensier rinoval la paura (B)

> (Ah, it is hard to speak of what it was,
> that savage forest, dense and difficult,
> which even in recall renews my fear)[4]

Now, what was the middle term of the first *terza rima* has assumed the position of the first and last, so that "B" has appeared in all three possible positions. What has happened within this pattern that Dante sustains for more than 14,000 lines of the *Commedia*? The rhyme of the middle term has now become the rhyme of the first and last terms. My own sense is that this rhythm of rhyme is the pattern of learning itself, if not the fundamental pattern of psyche's motion both out and down. Or, to take one more step, it is the pattern of *the libidinal flow of the poem* as it moves both on the page and within us. Moreover, this pattern of motion reflects and represents the action of learning in its fundamental form. Let me try to explain this last observation.

The A—B—A rhyme scheme may just comprise a micro version of the hero's journey, which is to say, the movement of psychic energy itself in the learning journey, where

$$A = \text{Departure}$$
$$B = \text{Initiation, conflict, tension, confrontation, conversion}$$
$$A = \text{Return,}$$

which is not a return to A as one knew it, for the knowledge and experience of B has now transformed the Return A. Therefore, students journeying or pilgrimaging through a poem repeat this process in a series of spiralic cycles during a class. The terza rima is in this process a tangible manifestation of the spiralic energy flow between readers, poem and back again to readers. In this journey, I want to propose, one might think of the relation of the plot of a narrative and its deeper psychic action, in this way:

plot moves libido
as
the underlying action moves psyche

Plot is to the matter of the poem—what can be apprehended by one or more of the five senses—as the action is the mimetic psychic and energic equivalent of that plot. If such a postulate has value, and I hope the reader allows me this proposition, then perhaps the poem's mythos exists in the crossroads of this energy exchange between matter (plot) and psychic energy, libidinal force (action), for the action of a work cannot be discerned except by an act of imagination that intuits the presence of this force field beneath the surface of the action, giving it shape, guiding it and offering the work the *poiesis* of psyche that sustains it and allows it the elasticity to accept many variations of reading while itself remaining undamaged and intact.

To give this interchange or transaction between the mythos of the readers and the mythos buried deep in the work, giving it form, I find it helpful in teaching to identify the extroverts and introverts in the room. After identifying them, I attempt to modulate—even mute at times!—the extroverts, and to motivate or coax the introverts to speak. I believe such action is important because the introverted psyche offers a different reading of the poem than does the extroverted: both are valuable, both are insightful, but too much extroverted reading uncovers only one slice of the mythos; too much introverted reading occludes other important slivers of the myth that governs the poem. The myth is always rumbling underground when it is activated in the dual acts of reading and then discussion. For it, like the variety of myths in the room, wishes to be heard. I imagine it this way: the poet serves as a midwife who assisted in the birth of that infant myth into the poem, where it has gestated, sometimes for centuries. That same mythos is born anew in each reading/rereading, and in subsequent discussions. Think here of class discussion as a rite of passage in reading closely a number of specific passages. The rite of reading stirs the myth, coaxes it to the surface, there to change and be changed by the participants—priestesses and priests of the printed word.

C. G. Jung is extremely observant of the canalization of libidinal energy flow. What his insights evoke in me is how the power of a narrative has the capacity to change the flow of libidinal energy in the reader, even to increase it. I have, for example, as a teacher, been surprised at the mystery that attends the end of most of my classes. After standing, moving about, writing on a chalkboard, gesturing, engaging in hyperbolic movements for 7 hours, I am left at the end of the class with more, not less energy. Often my legs ache, but I feel robust, not exhausted. Of course, all that changes about 2 hours after the class ends. But it is gravity, not grace, that pulls me down.

My sense is, following Jung's observations on "psychic energy," that inhabiting a symbolic world for that length of time nourishes both body and soul, augments its energy flow and increases one's joy in the presence of abundance. I am beginning to imagine symbols, poetic symbols, archetypal symbols in this way: they are akin to *energy transfer or exchange stations*; a symbol coalesces at that juncture where libido experiences a transfer of psychic values from one content to another. By extension, the classroom is like a conversion station in its own rite. Here, libidinal energy is transferred back and forth—progression and regression—person to poem to persons and back again, in very much the terza rimic behavior of Dante's poem. Such an understanding makes of the poem a living matter-energy field and flow. The degree of energy flow between the work and me is witnessed in the consequence of the degree of meaning that derives from the experience.

So we watch for the white whale to breach in all its majestic energy surge that lifts it forth from the water, where it suspends itself for a moment in mid-air. In that moment we contemplate its shimmering skin before it plunges once more below the water line of consciousness, perhaps leaving in its wake a footprint on the water's thin-skinned surface; there for a moment a calmness steals over the waters, a point of meditative stillness, lasting only a few moments, before that water is again reclaimed by the roiling sea's roll. The ship from which we view such a dazzling display are the decks of the classroom itself, a Pequod of the imagination, sailing serenely over the hissing waters of meditation and musings, seeking always a new tack on an old voyage, so ancient as to be full of the novelty of new discoveries in the yawl of such a pattern.

Notes

[1] Herman Melville, "Letter of Herman Melville to Nathaniel Hawthorne, 1 June, 1851," *The Letters of Herman Melville*, ed. Merell R. David and William Gilman (New Haven: Yale UP, 1960), p. 126.
[2] James Hillman, "On Culture and Chronic Disorder," in *City and Soul*, ed. Robert J. Leaver. Vol. 2 of The Uniform Edition of the Writings of James Hillman (Putnam, Conn., Spring Publications, Inc., 2006), p. 137.
[3] Dante Alighieri, *Inferno. The Divine Comedy*, trans. Allen Mandelbaum, introd. by Eugenio Montale (New York: Knopf, 1984), p. 59.
[4] Ibid.

SPIRITUAL RESONANCE IN THE CLASSROOM

Christopher M. Bache

It started this way. I was giving a lecture in one of my courses when a student asked a question. This was many years ago when I was a young professor fresh out of graduate school. I can't remember which course it was or the student, but what happened next is engraved in my memory. It was an ordinary question, one that I had fielded numerous times in previous semesters. On this particular day, however, instead of giving the answer that immediately popped into my mind, I stopped for a moment to mull over the possibilities. There was a pause in the flow of my thinking, a break in continuity as I asked myself: "Which answer has the best chance of getting through to this particular student?" Suddenly, I had a visual image of a small door in the back of my mind. The door opened and a slip of paper came through it with a suggestion written on it, an answer I had never used before. A different slant on a familiar topic. I tried it and it worked. In fact, it worked exceptionally well. Not only was the student satisfied, new ideas were sparked in the room. Learning had happened.

People experience these creative moments in different ways, but this is how I often experience them—a pause, a letting go, an emptiness, and a little door opening in the back of my mind. That was almost thirty years ago and intuition was less studied then than it is today, and even today many of my colleagues would raise their eyebrows at this story. We are, after all, rational people, highly trained professionals with advanced degrees, and rational people (with advanced degrees) don't have little doors in the back of their minds. I was a product of respected universities, well trained in research and dialectic, and not once in my many years of graduate education had anyone spoken to me about intuition, about how it worked or how to work with it in my teaching. But here it was.

In the beginning, I barely noticed these moments. Being a conscientious academic, I came to class with reams of carefully prepared notes and outlines to put on the board. I worked my students hard, covering the material thoroughly and conscientiously (I still do). In those early years, as soon as a student asked me a question, my memory banks would kick in and automatically generate the "correct answer." I didn't yet appreciate that there are a dozen versions of the "correct answer," each with a different nuance, a different emphasis, and from among all these possibilities there is one answer that is perfectly shaped to unlock this particular mind. Gradually I came to see that these moments were choice points, opportunities for intuition to transform an otherwise predictable lecture into a lively improvisational exchange tuned to a specific audience.

So I learned to work with these moments. I found that if I slowed down when asked a question and took the time, the door would appear and little pieces of imaginary paper would be passed to me from some deeper place with suggestions written on them: an idea, a picture, an example. I found that if I took the risk and used these gifts, some of which seemed strangely off target at the time, something magical would happen. Something new and unexpected would come forward. My answers seemed to hit the mark or ignite a vigorous conversation. Like that solid "whack" when you make perfect contact with a well-thrown pitch, the ideas that emerged often triggered a "perfect moment" in the classroom. The energy in the room would rise, students would brighten up, and we would move together in a creative excursion instead of in a predictable loop.

Now you may think that this was just an instance of a boring lecturer getting away from his scripted notes and maybe it was, but I don't think so. I've always loved teaching and I've always had the gift of gab. I know how to work a room, how to pace an audience and take them through the material in a way that builds to peaks and crescendos. This was something different. This was about cooperating with some mysterious process that brought out what was inside me in a way that was exceptionally fine-tuned to my audience. So for the next five years I experimented with these moments and learned how to weave them into my lectures. I learned how to integrate my prepared material with the novelty they unleashed. Then something new began to happen.

About the time I was jumping my first major academic hurtle, applying for tenure and moving from assistant to associate professor, students began coming up to me after class, when the room had emptied and they were sure no one would hear them, and saying things like: "You know, it's strange you used the example you did in class today, because that's exactly what happened to me this week." Sometimes it was: "That's exactly what happened to my Mom recently" or some other close family member.

The first time this happened, I thought it was interesting but shrugged it off. Then it happened a second and third time. In the years that followed it became a not uncommon occurrence. Not that it would happen every time I lectured, thank God, but it happened often enough that I couldn't dismiss it. Students were finding pieces of their personal lives showing up in my lectures in ways that startled them, sometimes jolting them. If my colleagues would have raised their eyebrows at the story of the little door in my mind, you can imagine what they would have done with this. So being a rational person (with advanced degrees), I kept it to myself. But it kept happening, just often enough to force me to pay attention to it.

An Example

This example comes from a public lecture I gave in Minneapolis a few years ago. In it I happened to mention as an aside that a number of students who were mothers have told me that they felt their babies had named themselves, that their incoming children had somehow communicated to them during the pregnancy their wish to be given a particular name. This usually took place in a dream or during a quiet meditative moment. In making this point, I said with some humor and a raised voice: "I don't want to be called Shirley; I want to be named . . ." (leaving the sentence unfinished). The line drew the expected chuckle from the room and we went on.

The choice of the name Shirley was entirely random for me. I don't remember ever talking about children naming themselves before in my lectures, and I certainly had never used the name Shirley before. I don't personally know any Shirleys, and there are no Shirleys in my family. However, my "random" comment struck a nerve with someone in the audience, an elderly lady in her 70's. She later took the trouble to write me a letter about it.

After telling me a bit about her family history, she mentioned the Shirley-line and said it had struck a chord with her. Her name was Shirley, but all her life she had felt that Shirley wasn't her "real" name. In her heart she was Dorothy. All her life she had secretly identified with the name Dorothy, though she did not share this with others. Then she went on to write:

> *About 25 years ago, when I was a juvenile probation officer in Minneapolis, I passed one of our referees in the hall. At that time, he was also Clerk of Court for our county. Harold said, "Hi, Dorothy." Then he quickly apologized and said, "I made that mistake because you and Dorothy D. started work the same week." That fact was true - but ever since that day, many, many people have said to me, "Hi, Dorothy." They are people I know well or people I've never met (for example, an attorney who called to discuss a case), etc. There have been times when I was introduced to someone as Shirley - and the person to whom I was introduced has turned around and introduced me to another, saying, "Meet Dorothy."*

Shirley felt that in her case her mother did not get the message. Though she had been named Shirley, she felt that she still gave off a Dorothy "vibe" that other people sometimes picked up on unconsciously.

A coincidence? Perhaps. Certainly another unusual story. Being a well-read person, Shirley interpreted the episode in terms of C. G. Jung's concept of synchronicity. Synchronicity is the idea that two events can be meaningfully connected even though they are not causally connected by any physical medium that we have identified. She felt a connection between my choice of the name Shirley in my throw-away line and the deep ambivalence she had carried all her life about having been named Shirley, and it had led her to get more engaged in my presentation.

The Magic

When these things first started happening in my classes, I was shocked because I was completely unaware of making any "paranormal" contact with my students, if you want to call it that, and certainly had not intended any. In fact, I had always thought of myself as something of a psychic brick incapable of such things. Nevertheless, the trickle of such reports grew until these synchronistic coincidences became a not uncommon occurrence in my classes. The students also began to tell me that it was uncanny how often my lectures answered, as if on cue, questions they were feeling but were not asking out loud.

Not only were students finding pieces of their lives in my lectures, but as the examples given above illustrate, these events often touched sensitive areas in their lives. It was as though a radar was operating below the threshold of our awareness that zeroed in on some part of their life that was hurting or constricted. Sometimes it touched a question they had been holding for a long time or triggered an insight they had been searching for, something they needed to find before they could take the next step in their lives. Sometimes it lanced a private pain that had been festering inside them for years. It was as if their souls were slipping messages to me, giving me hints on how I might reach them—telling me where they were hiding, where they were hurting, and, most importantly, what ideas they needed in order to take the next step in their development. This process, whatever it was, was obviously intelligent and obviously collective.

At home I started to call this mysterious interweaving of minds "the magic." When the magic happened, the walls of our separate minds seemed to come down temporarily, secrets were exchanged, and healing flowed. When the magic happened, my students and I tapped into levels of creativity beyond our separate capacities. On a good day the room was so filled with new ideas that after class I, too, copied down the blackboard. In these elevated conversations, I would sometimes catch glimpses of a deeper trajectory of ideas coming forward and working themselves out in our dialogue.

As you can imagine, these occurrences often affected my students deeply. Imagine that you are an undergraduate taking a class simply looking for some new ideas and three more credits toward your degree when suddenly the professor uses your recent history to illustrate a point he is making. Buried in the back of the room, safely anonymous in the crowd, suddenly your life is exposed, your heart pierced by words that seem aimed directly at you. Given such a personal invitation, how could you not sit up and pay attention? How could you not get more deeply involved in the course?

Spiritual Practice

Now I need to put another piece of the puzzle on the table, a piece that brings us to the very heart of the issue this essay raises. For as long as I've been an academic, I've also been a spiritual seeker. Sometimes I think of these as my two jobs: one I get paid for, the other is volunteer work. In my paid daytime job, I'm a university professor in a department of philosophy and religious studies. My work is education; my tools are reason, critical reflection, oratory, lots of reading, and a sense of humor. In my unpaid nighttime job, I'm a spiritual practitioner. Here the tools are silence, prayer, meditation, and, from time to time, immersion in deep, introspective, cathartic states of consciousness.

Spirituality is distinct from institutionalized religion, of course, but because the two sometimes get conflated, let me clarify what I mean by spiritual practice. As I understand it, spiritual practice is about cultivating an experiential opening to the larger patterns of life and the deeper roots of one's existence. It is not primarily about faith, creeds, or ritual, though these may play a role in one's practice. Pragmatically, spiritual practice systematically engages the constrictions within one's heart, mind, and body that keep awareness trapped within the narrow, repetitive cycles that constitute the private self, allowing one's being to relax into its deeper currents and its innate purity and eventually to open to the crystalline clarity that is the ever-present context and source of all experience. As this opening unfolds, one discovers many insights, encounters many truths, but the fundamental movement is simply to experience life as it is, in its fullness and immediacy, free of the constriction of self-reference.

When one experiences life as it is—in its "suchness" as the Zen Buddhists say or as a "grace" as the Christians say—one is inevitably struck by its wholeness, by the fact that at this profound and utterly simple level, life is not divided into parts. The things that usually fascinate us–the countless objects dangling in store windows or catalogued in our encyclopedias, the people walking down the street each with their different story—all these cease to exist as isolated, separate phenomena. Underneath and within this rich diversity, life lives and breathes as One. Its inherent wholeness is not fragmented by its emerging diversity. The essence of spirituality, at least as I understand and try to practice it, is to open to this living Oneness in which all "selves" become transparent to the splendor, the beauty, and the simplicity of the living Totality. This Totality or Oneness subsumes all distinctions. Wholeness, therefore, is the essence of the art. I hope other practitioners will feel their own experience echoed in this description.

Now let's return to our story. Honoring the time-tested wisdom of keeping one's personal beliefs and experiences out of the classroom, I kept my two jobs separate. I did not talk about my spiritual practice in my classes and revealed my personal convictions only rarely. My university job is not to instruct students in what I personally believe and certainly not to try to interest them in my particular spiritual path; rather, it is to expose them to some of the best minds in the intellectual and spiritual traditions I am responsible for teaching in our curriculum. While my spiritual practice has no doubt influenced what questions I think are deserving of my students' time and attention and what books are worthy of study, the choices I make always have to pass academic muster. Every course one puts into the college curriculum is carefully screened by several committees of one's peers, every syllabus is reviewed by one's department chair.

As a matter of professional ethics, therefore, I did not speak about my spiritual practice to my students, and yet with the passage of time I discovered that these two worlds I had kept apart so carefully were beginning to interact. As my spiritual practice deepened through the years, the synchronistic events I've been describing became more frequent and more intense. Despite my best effort to keep these two sides of my life separate from each other, they seemed to be reaching out and touching one another. Not only were the synchronicities increasing, but students were beginning to have unusually deep experiences around the concepts I was presenting in class. It was as though their lives were being activated by more than just the ideas, as though they were somehow being touched by the actual experience of these realities that now lived in me to some degree because of my practice.

Deepening Resonance

It took years before I was able to admit what now looks to me like the obvious and simple conclusion—that my spiritual practice outside of class was somehow sparking what was happening inside my classroom, not by my talking about it but silently, covertly, energetically. The expansive states of conscious emerging in my private life seemed to be triggering incidents of sympathetic resonance in my public life. The transpersonal states I was entering at home seemed to be activating the trans-individual fabric of life around me, energizing the meridians of the collective psyche and triggering a collective intelligence that was latent in my classroom.

My life and the lives of my students seemed to be moving in synch with each other. I remember one particular incident that dramatized this pattern. One night I had a dream that involved one of my students; it was a complex dream that did not make any sense to me. On my way to work, I decided that if this particular student showed up at my office hours that day, I would share the dream with her; otherwise I would let it go. (That's how cavalier I had gotten about these things.) Well, the student did show up, and she wanted to tell me about a dream she had had that same night in which I had been a player. When she told me her dream, I realized that our two dreams formed two halves of a larger whole. By themselves, the two half-dreams made little sense, but when we put them together, the resulting whole-dream did make sense, and it contained a significant message for her. The whole-dream was not about her and me, and there was nothing romantic going on between us. I had simply been enlisted to help her unconscious communicate a point to her conscious awareness. When she left my office that day she had much to think about, and I moved on to what came next. Something was always coming up next.

These synchronicities became particularly pronounced during a period of several years when I was undergoing a series of powerful inner experiences in my practice that were breaking me down at very deep levels. All spiritual traditions describe a phase of interior work that involves dissolving the membrane that exists between self and other. They describe a membrane or domain that marks the boundary between the individual and the surrounding universe, the interface of the personal and the transpersonal psyche. On the near side of this membrane, the world appears to be composed of separate beings, each with their own private existence. On the far side of the membrane, the world appears as an integrated whole, a continuum of energy that eventually shows itself to be a massive, unfathomably complex, extravagantly beautiful, integrated single life form. Hence, this boundary membrane is the domain of "death and rebirth," death to the world of the private self and rebirth into a larger transcendental order that underlies life's diversity. When a practitioner is transitioning through this territory, standing at the interface of these two paradoxically compatible realities, powerful synchronicities with other persons sometimes manifest.

As my inner work came to focus on this boundary, as it does sooner or later for every practitioner, some of my students seemed to be simultaneously undergoing particularly difficult challenges in their own lives. Most of my students did not enter these waters, of course, and passed through my courses untouched by these dynamics. But some did enter them. Those who did sometimes felt themselves coming to a breaking point in their lives or a moment of supreme risk-taking. It was as though they and I were together being drawn through a giant death-rebirth vortex, a vortex that was breaking all of us down in different ways, uprooting deeply buried pains, and crushing restrictive barriers in our lives.

Eventually, I realized the fact that my inner and my outer life, my "private" spiritual practice and my public professional life, could not be kept entirely separate from each other was demonstrating an important truth about the nature of consciousness and the deep structure of reality. It was actually demonstrating the validity of one of the core axioms of the perennial perspective: the inherent wholeness of existence the integrated, interpenetrating nature of the universe. Beneath the surface of appearances there are energetic exchanges that connect our lives to those around us, subtle threads that weave our lives into larger wholes. From one perspective consciousness is clearly differentiated into separate lives, and yet from this deeper perspective it functions holistically, pulsing with a deeper intentionality that ignores the boundaries between self and other.

Though I left my spiritual practice at home every morning when I went to the university, I could not leave myself at home, and my spiritual practice seemed to be changing my energetic constitution at deep levels. It appeared that my "private" attempt to know and actualize a more authentic existence and deeper communion with life was causing my person to act as a kind of lightning rod triggering sparks of a similar awakening among those students who were receptive to this influence. And this was happening automatically, without conscious intention or direction on my part.

I understand how strange this story is likely to sound to readers who, like me, were educated to think of the mind as compartmentalized and physically constrained to the brain. Yet, I believe that this conventional way of thinking is simply false, and it does educators a great disservice because it desensitizes us to the subtler collective textures of the teaching experience. By failing to legitimate our lived-experience, it obstructs our ability to make sense of what is actually taking place in our classroom and thus stifles the full transformative potential of the student-teacher relationship. It is not that people's minds don't function separately in a "stand alone" mode, because they obviously do, but it appears that this is not the whole truth. There is also a more subtle dynamic operating in the classroom, a collective dynamic that reflects the wavelike features of mind that transcend and integrate the particle-like mind, a collective intelligence that surrounds our personal intelligence.

If there is an insight that my students and I wish to share with the reader that comes from our experience, it is this. If you are an educator who has chosen a form of spiritual practice that has the capacity to activate deep levels of the unconscious, you can expect to stimulate sympathetic resonances in at least some of your students. Separate minds are an illusion of the senses, how life appears if you look at it through only one eye. If you begin to immerse yourself in the inherent wholeness of life and to stimulate the purification processes that inevitably occur when self seeks True Self, you will not make this journey alone. As an educator, you must anticipate that at least some of your students will move in rhythm with your descent. You must expect it and you must prepare for it. Like ripples on water, these resonances are inevitable. And the better teacher you are, the more powerful you can expect them to be.

POETIC AWARENESS: IMAGINING AND THE EXPERIENCE OF SOUL

Matthew Green

Goodbye, said the fox. And now here is my secret, a very simple secret:
It is only with the heart that one can see rightly;
what is essential is invisible to the eye.
~Antoine de Saint-Exupéry[1]

Stepping into a setting like Mission Santa Barbara or the ancient site of Delphi or looking out onto a field of sunflowers or a towering waterfall, we might readily glimpse the subjectivity of the landscape. Our sensory perception is engaged; our emotions are heightened. The place speaks to us as if alive. We can sense its depth in its grandeur and imposing forms, in the vibrant colors, in the cool, weathered surfaces, and in evocative sounds and smells. Through the tangible and visible features of a place, of an encounter, we sense and connect with an invisible subjectivity, turning event into experience of soul, as James Hillman expresses it.[2]

We might take for granted the ability to adopt such a perspective in an encounter. And yet, it is not one readily recognized or articulated in Western society. Even less is it formulated and taught as a basic skill in our schools and in other learning settings. Imagine teachers educating their students, from the preschooler to the older adult learner, in the mode of knowing of the heart—the mode of knowing by means of which we apprehend the subjective *other* in each encounter and thus experience the poetic dimension that is soul in its depth, connection, meaningfulness—in the world around us! This mode of knowing I call *poetic awareness.*

I discovered early on in my tenure as director and teacher for a college Study Abroad program, primarily in France, that developing poetic awareness was essential to the students' education. I observed that it was not what the students learned about the country, how many famous places they visited, or even how much fun they had that generally made the experience meaningful to them. Students instead spoke of how much they were changed and how affected they were by the world they encountered. What gave meaning was getting to know and coming to love an aspect of the world that before had been foreign, distant, even threatening. I was eventually able to identify poetic awareness as the element behind the students' capacity to know and to be in relationship with the world they encountered in its specificity. It was the capacity to engage the world with the heart, to pause and enter into an encounter through its images that gave a sense of meaning and soul to their experience.

I eventually came to consider learning about France, indeed the entire project of study abroad, as a pretext for learning to engage the world with poetic awareness. While I valued and very much enjoyed teaching French language and culture, it was clear to me that poetic awareness and the experience of soul had to be central in my teaching and in the students' learning. Otherwise, I could never have persisted in study abroad. Attention to poetic awareness gave expression to soul both as an aspect of the *process* of teaching (and learning) and as a feature of *what* the students learned and took away from their stay abroad. I suspect that teachers lose their passion and energy for teaching not only because of the workload, the conditions, and pressures of the job but also because their teaching and the students' learning do not intentionally involve them in the experience of soul. At some point absence of soul, in teaching as in life, becomes unbearable; indeed, I sense that it is the root of the unbearable lightness of being that so many of us experience in Western society. For the fifteen years I was in France, I was constantly engaged in figuring out how teaching French language and culture could also involve teaching poetic awareness. In this essay, I draw on that experience to offer a number of reflections regarding such a form of teaching.

I should acknowledge at the outset that I do not assume on the part of teacher (or student) an understanding or even an awareness of soul or of knowing that is based in imagining. Little in the training of teachers reveals a concern for the experience of soul as a feature of a learning instructional program. I do not believe, however, that this lack of awareness or concern reflects an absence of interest in matters of soul on the part of teachers. I have had conversations with many from numerous disciplines and schools; their reaction to even a brief introduction to this idea of soul and its relevance in learning is generally one of enthusiasm and curiosity. It seems that there is a thirst for an alternative to the objectivism and disembodied learning that dominates our society.

For teachers to be able to bring the heart's mode of knowing into their teaching and their students' learning, however, they must first develop a clear understanding of and appreciation for this perspective. It is not enough for teachers to understand poetic awareness as a concept. Being able to define it and present it in a lesson will not do much to further the learning and practice of soul in the classroom. The idea has to be understood as a gnosis, as a felt and lived reality and truth. To reach this level of understanding takes earnest grappling with the notion of soul and its mode of knowing.

In his book, *The Thought of the Heart and Soul of the World*, Hillman proposes the expression *imaginational intelligence* for the mode of knowing that involves us in soul: "Imaginational intelligence resides in the heart; intelligence of the heart is a simultaneous knowing and loving by means of imagining."[3] When knowing is based in imagining—hosting and responding to the images that emerge in an encounter—knowing involves loving, that is, experiencing a sense of meaningfulness, connection, and participation. When the heart is engaged, the world is no longer perceived solely in terms of objective, physical reality; it is also apprehended as image. Images are spontaneous expressions of soul, Hillman[4] has observed, drawing on Jung; they manifest an event in its depth and in its subjectivity. Poetic awareness, which is another way of naming the intelligence of the heart, allows us to see in and through the visible, sensory qualities of an encounter to the invisible images that erupt in the psyche to reveal its depth and interiority. With poetic awareness, we encounter an image and thus experience it as an expression of soul.

A particular setting comes to mind here. Imagine coming upon a mist or haze-covered landscape—for example, a low-lying light mist blanketing a bucolic river valley. Because we cannot see the landscape enough to define it empirically, our senses throw themselves beyond the visible and images rush in to "complete the picture." As images engage our attention, they inevitably evoke an aesthetic response, which connects us affectively to the setting or to elements of the encounter. Such is the nature of an image; it animates the heart. The heart comes alive with a sense of wonder and enchantment, in this case precisely because the landscape does not offer certainties or explanations. Linear perception at this moment of encounter yields to perceiving with the heart. Images could emerge in any encounter, but we are not always able or inclined to suspend the literal, objective mind and its way of engaging and knowing the world in order to sufficiently host them in our imagining.

We might now better understand the secret the fox shares with the little prince: "Only with the heart can one see rightly; what is essential is invisible to the eye."[5] "What is essential" is the invisible realm of image that we see only with the heart. It is with the imagining of the heart that we know mystery, wonder, and awe and that we acknowledge and respond to the beauty and the spirit of place in a particular landscape. It is with the heart that we become attached to and find meaningful what we once perceived and experienced as insignificant, strange, or intolerable. The dank, sketchy café that a student would disparage and avoid at all costs at the start of a term becomes the endearing hangout because of engagement in the heart's imagining. It is by means of the heart's imagining that we cross the invisible boundaries that separate us from the multitude of worlds around us and from the unlimited possibilities present in each encounter.

Another way to approach understanding poetic awareness is to consider that soul is an encounter between an animated landscape and an imagining self. Poetic awareness, from this perspective, has to do with recognizing in each landscape a world ensouled—*anima mundi*—the "soul of the world." The visible forms and features bespeak of an invisible dimension, the interior image of an event. This is to say that the literal, visible features of an encounter also speak as poetic expression, as metaphor. Recovering poetic awareness as a mode of knowing returns the invisible poetic dimension that is *anima mundi* to our encounters.

In the literature of archetypal psychology and ecopsychology, there are references to a number of qualities that call attention to an animated, ensouled world. Among these are beauty, nature, spirit of place, patterns, story, and the ugly. It is not hard to see how each of these qualities, which I describe elsewhere in detail,[6] awakens our imaginational engagement. Beauty, for example, is a quality in the world that readily elicits imaginational participation. Hillman suggests that one way we recognize relational qualities in the world is precisely through the lure of beauty: "Each of us knows that nothing so affects the soul, so transports it, as moments of beauty—in nature, a face, a song, an action or dream. . . . These moments are therapeutic in the truest sense: they make us aware of soul and make us care for its value."[7] Soul speaks through beauty: it speaks to the senses and awakens and enlivens our sense of delight, wonder, and awe. We experience beauty not simply as a visible feature but as that which readily becomes image, that is, that animates the imagination.

Similarly, encounters with nature and spirit of place can also draw us out of ourselves and into dialogue with images and the subjective otherness in the landscape, which for the time of the encounter, at least, makes us intimately aware of soul. This list—beauty, nature, spirit of place, patterns, story, and the ugly—represents one way of delineating qualities in the world that readily allows us, or prompts us, to recognize and engage the depth and subjectivity of an event. We might begin with this list to more deeply understand the idea of poetic awareness and to consider contexts for introducing our students to this mode of knowing. In our teaching, we might eventually use other language and uncover additional ways to evoke the poetic qualities that we encounter in the world.

Each encounter, while presenting to our senses relational qualities, is also asking us, compelling us, to participate. We participate by means of our imagining. Without the engagement of the imagination, poetic qualities in the landscape, even beauty and nature, strike us as inanimate. The landscape remains a flatland, to use the expression of Ken Wilber's. Poetic awareness, as a mode of knowing, is a simultaneous movement of awareness outward into an encounter (as animated landscape and expression of soul) and inward into the dynamics of imagining in the psyche (the personal, interior self).

We need to understand that the imagining involved in poetic awareness is not singular but reflects instead a differentiated imagination—various ways that we invite, host, and respond to images that emerge in an encounter. The genius of Hillman's insight into soul, in my appreciation of his work, is especially evident in his reflections on the act of imagining. He speaks of imagining, for example, in terms of aesthetic response: *notitia* or attentive noticing, digesting an image, personifying, psychologizing, pathologizing, mythologizing, historicizing. These ideas are amply developed in his book *Re-Visioning Psychology*.[8] Each of these responses evokes a different way we engage soul in an encounter by means of its images. It is beyond the scope of this essay to elaborate on these and other modes of the heart's imagining. It is important to recognize, however, that in this context imagining is understood as an activity of soul. Hillman has, in fact, observed that "the primary activity of the psyche [soul] is imagining."[9] It is by means of our imagining that we experience the poetic qualities of an event.

It is problematic that in education, and in our culture in general, imagining and the imagination are primarily understood as limited to creative thinking (or problem-solving) and imaginary thinking (or fantasy). And yet, imagination as an activity of soul cannot be equated with either, although it certainly involves both creative thinking and fantasy. How we understand the imagination, of course, shapes what and how we teach in the name of imagination. Until we also consider the imagination as a mode of knowing that involves engaging images as an activity of the heart, the programs that we offer in our schools designed to foster the imagination will only superficially or accidentally prepare students to consciously engage the world with soul and to experience the world as soul.

I present this brief introduction to poetic awareness while well aware that learning *about* this mode of knowing is distinct from learning to engage it in an encounter with the world. It is my sense that learning it as a concept does not necessarily facilitate its practice. The concern of the teacher is not to ensure that students know *about* poetic awareness but, rather, that they learn to engage their world *with* poetic awareness.

In my own teaching, it became evident that poetic awareness is not so much learned as it is imposed. It is imposed in that we are awakened or shocked into the heart's mode of knowing through encounters that prompt our imagining. Such learning happens not in a linear, rational progression but, rather, in quantum shifts in awareness. Learning poetic awareness essentially involves becoming conscious of the heart's mode of knowing as we engage it (in moments that command our attention). It is when we are shocked out of our habitual ways of engaging the world and forced to reimagine it that we enter a context, a liminal space, that holds the potential for awakening the imagining heart as well as our consciousness of this imagining. This recognition, of course, is as much the case for teachers learning this mode of knowing as it is for students. How we experience these shocks, in what setting, to what intensity, what language and ideas we use to speak of and imagine them, how we prepare for, process, and understand them determine how likely it is they will prompt an expanded capacity to engage in poetic awareness. The challenge facing a teacher is to develop and implement a learning program that accounts for these various capacities in students.

The primary means of teaching and learning poetic awareness is the *encounter*. It takes just such an experience to reveal the quality of students' imaginational engagement with the world. In the Study Abroad program, for example, without the students' encounters with French society, there would have been no object or "raw material" with which to address or work on the quality of their engagement with the world. Students learn poetic awareness when they are invited to engage in an encounter and then are asked to reflect on their experience in dialogue with others. (For students to accept this dialogue, poetic awareness must be an explicit or, at least, implicit objective of learning.)

For some time, I thought that only actual encounters—with people, landscapes, objects—could serve to teach poetic awareness. My focus was on learning associated with my students' encounters with the French people and their culture. I now appreciate, especially after considering Parker Palmer's reflections on subject-centered teaching,[10] that encounters also happen with the subject of study itself. When a subject is considered alive and not simply an inanimate object of knowledge, then a meaningful relationship with it becomes possible. I would suggest, nevertheless, that encounters with the world merit special consideration since they especially facilitate poetic awareness: they magnify both the necessity and exposure of a student's imaginational engagement in an encounter.

Also essential to awakening a student's awareness of her imaginational response in an encounter is the teacher's participation as *witness,* that is, as an external observer to reflect back images that reveal in what ways the student's lack of imaginational engagement might be limiting her experience. The teacher's (and fellow students') observations help the student to recognize visible features in the encounter that she did not notice as well as to explore invisible qualities, "animated possibilities," that she may not have apprehended or imagined. In the interaction, the teacher also helps the student identify and confront the attitudes, opinions, and behaviors that are most blatantly limiting her imaginational engagement *and* that she is most ready and able to address. The dilemma is that certain fundamental aspects of *who the student is* are often judged out of bounds or irrelevant by the education community: teachers, students, administrators, and parents. It is considered taboo and sometimes even dangerous for teachers to address a student's personal dimension in their teaching. Teaching poetic awareness, however, necessarily involves witnessing; teachers need to be able to effectively identify and mirror back to students those aspects of their participation in encounters and in learning that most limit their engagement in soul. The aspects most limiting students' engagement in soul have everything to do with the personal dimension.

For example, a student relating what she learned about French village culture from a two-week encounter with a village would inevitably reveal elements of her curiosity of this world, her tolerance for the rural, rustic, even rudimentary quality of the village, and her inclination to perceive and engage subtle and unfamiliar features of village life. The personal dimension of attitudes and behaviors directly impacts the quality and scope of the student's experiences on which she bases her observations (and learning). The teacher must address—that is, witness or mirror back to the student—this dimension in order to help her learn to fully engage and thus learn from the village.

An equally important component of teaching poetic awareness is the language and conceptual framework the teacher uses to introduce this perspective. The terminology and ideas must somehow provide an environment and approach that both value and stimulate this mode of knowing, expressing it in a way that naturally fits into the subject area of the class. I recognize that in most settings the language and ideas used to teach a sensibility of soul would not readily allow for the word *soul* or easily integrate the specific language and ideas of depth psychology. Ideally, the teacher would formulate the perspective of poetic awareness using language and concepts that are not only consistent with his or her particular discipline and particular learning setting but that also are drawn specifically from the discipline. Teachers of music and the arts can naturally draw from writings on aesthetic appreciation as well as promote participatory knowing. However, we need not limit the teaching of poetic awareness to the arts. Science, for example, also produces a literature that is rich in reflections on participatory knowing.

Because t the Study Abroad program was set in a foreign culture and had an explicit objective of promoting cultural sensitivity— sensitivity to differences in culture or subculture—much of the language and conceptual framework were drawn from intercultural communication. Words, expressions, and ideas revealing a concern for soul and imagination, albeit in the language of intercultural communication and cross-cultural anthropology, emerged from readings, activities, discussions, and assignments. The language and ideas became the backdrop for individual and group interactions and as such both reflected and defined the underlying learning ambitions. Moreover, since the program took place in France, special language and ideas were also drawn from French literature and culture (such as from *The Little Prince*).

I can extend these reflections on teaching poetic awareness by way of example. The first activity of the Study Abroad program in France was called the "metro stop." This exercise, which always took place on the first full day in the country, introduced the approach to learning that marked the program as a whole.[11] In the activity, each student was given the name of a Paris metro station, along with four or five other words that had some association with the *quartier*, or neighborhood, surrounding the station. After a short briefing in which I introduced the concept of experience-based learning and the details of the task, I invited the students to find the way to *their* metro station and then to return five hours later to report on what they had learned about the words and places they had visited.

Now, imagine a student reporting back that the area surrounding her metro station was boring and unfriendly and that this inhospitality kept her from learning about her words or really discovering any details about the area. While acknowledging that the student's response may

117

indeed reflect qualities of the *quartier*, in the group discussion I would draw her attention to physical, sensory features in the encounter as well as to her aesthetic reactions to these features. I would also invite her to ponder features of the landscape that she had dismissed or neglected and to reconsider or reimagine her responses to certain elements of the encounter. In the discussion, this student would also likely hear reports from others who had encountered a face of Paris that was more hospitable and engaging. From such an exercise, repeated in different forms and configurations throughout a semester, a student might discover other ways of engaging in an encounter and begin to participate more deeply in the unlimited potential of her encounters— —the animated possibilities of soul. In this way, the student would learn to recognize and practice the mode of knowing that I have been calling poetic awareness.

From my experience, I have found that giving special consideration at the beginning of the program to encounters with features that especially claim imaginational attention facilitates the teaching and learning of poetic awareness. So many students today suffer from what Hillman refers to as *anesthesia*, a numbing of sensory perception and aesthetic response to image. I observed that when students anticipated an encounter with beauty or the spirit of a place, they were more disposed to engage the event with their senses and to host images that connected them affectively to the event (or with some aspect of it). One significant benefit of directing the program in France was that places of beauty abounded, as did settings and events with a palpable spirit or character. In the metro stop assignment, for example, students had encounters with places like Notre Dame, the Champs-Elysées, and La Tour Eiffel. Ideally, the energy behind the curiosity and interest that students brought to this first encounter fueled attentive noticing and imagining in the many "ordinary" encounters that followed. Finding settings and conditions that ignite students' inclination to enter into an encounter with an engaged imagination is an important aspect of teaching this mode of knowing.

I want to acknowledge two learning objectives active in the metro stop example. First, as I noted above, the student is asked to recognize that he plays an active role in the learning equation. He cannot remain a passive recipient of information; *how* he learns (that is, how he engages in and responds to the world) determines *what* he learns. This, of course, is also a fundamental premise behind the experience-based learning championed by John Dewey.[12] If learning is to emerge from an encounter, who the student is—the personal dimension he brings to the encounter—becomes an essential element in the learning equation. The necessity of such participation proves to be a considerable obstacle to teaching poetic awareness when so many students today are used to passively receiving information and ideas in a lecture or from a book or online, then being tested on how much they know or how well they can manipulate or think critically about the material presented. Learning from their own encounters is greeted as foreign and threatening, as is examining who they are as part of the learning process. Similarly, students (and even many teachers) do not readily accept it when learning arrangements allow learning content to be determined, to some extent, by an encounter itself. The implications of such an approach are far-reaching and bring into question the relevance and effectiveness of a fixed curriculum as well as of rigid content standards.

In the metro stop exercise, the objective of learning is not just to learn *about* Paris. More significant is for the student to learn about Paris through an *experience* of the city. True knowledge about the place, from the perspective of poetic awareness, needs to be anchored in an experience. Because the objective of the activity was as much to foster poetic awareness as it was to learn about Paris, in the discussion I generally gave as much, if not greater, attention to the quality of the student's experience as I did to the information about the *quartier* or to the words associated with the metro station.

Learning about Paris was, nevertheless, central to the exercise. I realized as I reflected on how to integrate a concern for poetic awareness into the Study Abroad program that poetic awareness could not be the primary objective of learning. For the student, the object of learning was to come to know an aspect of the world by means of a lived encounter. Poetic awareness was revealed to be the mode of this knowing. Any subject of study that involves encounters as an aspect of learning can integrate poetic awareness as a method and thus as a learning objective. Seen this way, poetic awareness is a basic skill that, much like critical thinking, can be taught and learned in most any subject.

Notes

[1] Antoine de Saint Exupéry, *The Little Prince*, trans. K. Woods (New York: Harcourt Brace Jovanovich), 73.

[2] James Hillman, *Re-Visioning Psychology* (New York: Harper & Row, 1975).

[3] James Hillman, *The Thought of the Heart and the Soul of the World* (Woodstock, CT: Spring Publications, 1982), 7.

[4] James Hillman, *Healing Fiction* (Woodstock, CT: Spring Publications, 1983).

[5] Antoine de Saint Exupéry, *The Little Prince*.

[6] Matthew Green, "Poetic Awareness: Imagination and Soul in Education" (Doctoral Dissertation, Pacifica Graduate Institute, 2007).

[7] James Hillman and Michael Ventura, *We've Had a Hundred Years of Psychotherapy and the World is Getting Worse* (San Francisco: HarperSan Francisco, 1992), 15.

[8] James Hillman, *Re-Visioning Psychology*.

[9] James Hillman and Michael Ventura, *We've Had a Hundred Years of Psychotherapy*, 62.

[10] Parker Palmer, *The Courage to Teach* (San Francisco: Jossey-Bass, 1998).

[11] The metro stop exercise, which was more commonly referred to as the "drop off," was a signature feature of the School for International Training (SIT), which sponsored the program in France. SIT is the educational division of World Learning Inc., an organization based in Vermont dedicated to international understanding.

[12] John Dewey, *Experience and Education* (New York: Macmillan, 1938).

"TILL WE HAVE FACES": IMAGE AS PSYCHE

Elizabeth Fergus-Jean

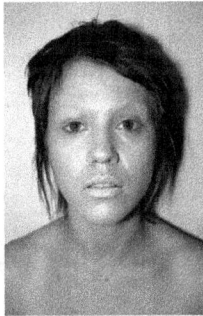

Erica Esham 2007

I saw well why the gods do not speak to us openly, nor let us answer. Till that word [which has lain at the center of one's soul for years] can be dug out of us, why should they hear the babble that we think we mean? How can they meet us face to face till we have faces?

~C. S. Lewis[1]

I have the joy and privilege of teaching a wide range of arts and humanities courses in a variety of venues. However, regardless of the diverse content and different types of students I encounter, there is one important constant that runs throughout any course I teach: a recognition of the impact and importance of *image*. What I have discovered in the classroom is that few students understand images to be anything other than captured surface reflections derived from contemporary experience. The effect of this narrow reading of image is profound. It allows the flattened cultural imagination of the media to use images as mere illustrations rather than understanding them mythopoetically. Images certainly can be illustrations of ideas; however, to limit them to such a narrow definition restricts their multivalent potentialities.

To counter this trend, it is important to incorporate an expanded understanding of image within the classroom and to clearly understand how image, specifically self-image, can lead to *informing* the individual and, through the process, to *transforming* the act of teaching itself. To illuminate this point I have included several examples of visual images created by my students' work in the Personal Mythology course I created for the Columbus College of Art and Design. I believe these self-portraits speak of the depth and power in giving voice to psyche in image; that is, they are embodiments of students' expanded relationship to self-awareness as evidenced in image.

Aaron Geiser 2005

Psyche Responds to Image

I begin by considering media uses of image, which directly influence the ways we understand image today. We are inundated by such imagery, which is predominately influenced by commercial motives. However, even in the midst of such stylized images, we are still awed by other more potent images that visit us in dreams; we also bear witness to our own inner stories as they are revealed in paintings, poems, and dance. These images entail psychic observation of our inner stories. This action of faithful witness is perhaps a function of a need for remembrance, illustrated by the growing number of individuals who are authorial image-makers of their own lives via the camera or camcorder. This essay, however, is not primarily concerned with acts of making images nor with the range of techniques associated with such making. Rather, the focus of this discussion involves several stages: finding self-image; engaging creatively with image as an extension of the archetypal self; and then expanding the nature of image within the classroom.

When one considers the multidimensional levels in culture and self conveyed via image and imaginal works, it seems essential to encourage students by expanding their sense of image through its dynamic relationships with their sense of self and with the world around them. A poignant example of the dynamic interplay of outer appearance and inner sense of self is exhibited in the self-portraits created by Media Studies student Brian Kellett.

Brian Kellett 2006

Brian's images reveal a tension between the certainty of his physical confinement and the expansiveness of his spirit. His situation as expressed by these images tells his story in his own voice. They can be seen as a triumph of his inner being, given significance by the act of image-making. In stark contrast, consider Brian's images in the context of the kinds of images *projected* onto us through the media as well as through cultural expectations. Such outer image-stories pushed upon us establish a nearly impenetrable wall of nonintegrated illusions that serve a further function: as a basis for corrosive meta-stories. An example of such media-encoded images can be seen in the "Campaign for Real Beauty" advertising campaign of the Dove Corporation. In "Evolution," a clip now available for viewing at their website, we watch as an ordinary young woman is literally transformed into a "beauty" through the application of make-up and high-tech computer manipulation.[2] This thirty-second ad reveals one way in which the media projects specific types of image-stories onto an unknowing public and then suggests they be imitated.

Through this example we see how a contemporary extension of image, rendered as a kind of mask to conceal true identity, can promote a pervasive societal message. Image thus becomes a servant to contain psyche rather than to reintegrate its elements. The consequence of such deception is that we are pushed further from our own lived experience by an onslaught of illustrative images telling us how we must look and feel, even extending to what we must own and do. Yet deep within ourselves we know these images do not authentically mirror our deeper-seated self-image. In terms of image as process, we are culturally sold a bill of goods that consistently supplies the wrong products for our psychic development.

It is important to recognize the quicksand of images we are immersed in. To do this I ask students to find predominantly embedded cultural stories as they are expressed in the media; I call the assignment, "It's Everywhere." In this exercise students devote one week to attending and gathering concepts and images found everywhere through media. Most students respond by bringing in advertisements selling various products. From our reflections during class discussions, what is often observed with much surprise is that the literal product in these images and texts isn't the only thing being sold. Students quickly begin to realize that within the image text, embedded preferences are substituted for alternative elements, such that preferences for very specific body types (and therefore preferred body images) are also being promoted and intrinsically aligned with a product. These inundations of image reflect current cultural meta-narratives aggressively projected onto our psyches. In sum, the pervasive image story told repeatedly is: if you look slim, beautiful, and perfect (with respect to embedded image codes), you will be part of the in-crowd and enjoy popularity and attention. However, since virtually no one naturally appears like the people in the ads, imagine the devastating impact such cultural stories level on one's personal story and self-image. Following such image texts often becomes an act of unrelenting and desperate questing for an unattainable, illusive, and ever-changing image, in its narrowest sense. We can clearly see the impact of such prescribed codes of beauty and cultural norms on self-image, as evidenced in the haunting self-portrait by Courtney Scott. In this image we see Courtney as she imagines herself—alone, in a vacant parking lot, with a character facemask drawn onto a shopping bag that hides herself.

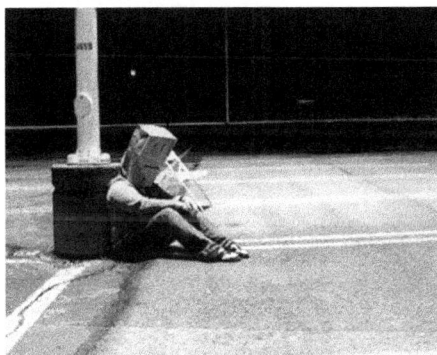

Courtney Scott 2003

Curiously, but not surprisingly, Courtney's state of mind is also a predominant theme of many reality TV shows—the transformation of "ordinary" people into semblances of models who appear in ads. In these presentations, a wide variety of "corrective" transformations are staged, often with a goal of offering participants opportunities to become millionaires, to meet the perfect alluring bachelor or bachelorette, or—in the extreme—to reconstitute one's selfhood with reconstructive surgery and cosmetic redefinition, as seen on such shows like *The Swan* and *Extreme Makeover.*

While for some this is merely diversionary entertainment, for others it is an ongoing treadmill of illusions, a recirculating nightmare that involves drastic and wholesale restructuring of self and psyche. As an example of how outer cosmetic changes can affect the inner proportions of self as sharply as a scalpel incises the psyche, consider the genesis of images of Michael Jackson before he began his series of plastic surgeries to the way he now appears.[3] From my point of view, the changes, detached from a holistic sense of self, are disturbing. He has literally effaced his self-image. In sum, it is a horrifying, nightmarish attack on oneself. If not proving the point, it at least certainly raises the question: is the exterior view of ourselves what matters most? Moreover, what must we sacrifice in our interior world in futile attempts to conform to these exterior images?

As a second movement into image, I encourage students to unveil and so expose these embedded cultural narratives and to critically reflect upon their creative personal responses to the meta-narratives. Specifically, these responses are also images, visual counterpoles to these stories, authored by the student and then given verbal dimension through discussion. I then ask them to share the emotional territories revealed when reflecting upon both sets of images. The essential and salient questions become: What impact have these images had on your psyche and on your developing narrative of self? Further, how have these narratives led you to define who you are in your heart? Do these images reflect your sense of values? Your ideals? And do they reflect your experience of being in the world?

Posing these fundamental questions helps students actively engage in discovering their own story and the story of their local and more encompassing cultures, through their increased awareness of the outer forces that frame image and the inner forces that give image life. Jenn Beck's self-portrait engages the power of the societal mask to obscure the inner self. The mask's obscuring power has gone awry, distorting all but her eyes, which are windows of the self within her that wishes to emerge and be truly witnessed.

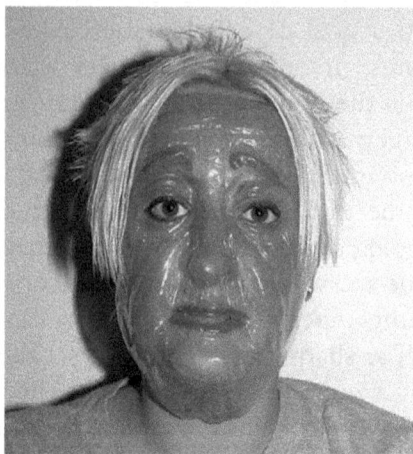

Jenn Beck 2005

Psyche is Image

C. G. Jung states that "psyche is image"; we might reverse his assertion and say "image is psyche." By extension this suggests that who we are is created largely via images: visual, sound, body, taste, smell, and even word images. Therefore, to discuss the fuller nature of image with students, I focus on its transcendent qualities and on its multivalent nature. Although many people want to fix specific meanings to images, whether in a painting or a dream image, in the psychic sense images are not so easy to pin down; they remain in large measure polysemous and thus open to various meanings and nuances.

Understood in their dynamic, transformative sense, images are more like fluid constructs and multivalent processes, but they are often misread as static objects. In truth, they are more like unfolding events. Therefore, each encounter with an image is a new experience. As such they are analogous to a stream into which one cannot step twice because the stream's movement makes it always new. In experiencing images differently insofar as we are in a state of change, each encounter with image is a new experience as well as an opportunity to create an evolving personal story.

Our capacity for vision is formed through our unique personal lenses. We use such lenses to make and engage all forms of perceived images, whether imaginary or real. Further, as our life flows into the future, so too must our relationship with an image change; that is, as our lives change, so too must our lenses. If we are no longer the person we once were, then how could we expect an image to remain stagnant?

It is very useful, therefore, to begin the process of realizing our personal vision by loosening our need for a specific meaning or understanding of an image, all the while realizing that our own understanding may very well differ from another's. Metaphorically we see all forms of images through different perceptual lenses. Our lenses can be imagined as multiple layers of acquired and inherited biases that distort our relationship to experience. Therefore, the basis for understanding any image and all that it embodies must include a recognition of the lens through which we perceive. Such a perspectival awareness is especially important for the works that students make, the ways in which they perceive others, and the images that are manifested in culture. Therefore, even when we share the same cultural background and perhaps even the same ancestral lineage, our personal lens is always unique to ourselves.

Anna Dickson's images speak eloquently of the healing power of an integrated personal lens, of the language of image, and the transformative process of allowing image to emerge from within. Her images are moving testaments to the healing power of expression.

Anna Dickson 2003

Till That Image Can Be Dug Out of Us

Within the classroom, reading the outer image a student projects is simply a surface scanning of codes: dress, traits, and mannerisms, to name a few attributes. What lies beneath the surface image can easily be overlooked but is essential to see, for therein lies the untold image-story: the self-image and imaginal lens through which individuals imagine their life story. It is this interior and often guarded self-image that we as teachers can help students begin to *see into*.

For students, the practice of directly *seeing into* self-images involves creativity, imagination, and actually peering *into* their personal, deeply seated formative process. This involves engagement of imagination and remembrance. As I assist students in becoming aware of their personal imaginal lenses, I at the same time enable them to better understand the role of lenses in forming both appearances and actions of images they encounter. For true seeing, whether literal or metaphorical, requires an individual to meld inner and outer lived experiences. Thus, recognition of one's lens involves remembrance of one's entire self and of one's self-image. The result of such a correspondence allows a similar reintegration of self into image. Such a profound remembering of self is evident in the self-portrait by Kate Morgan. In this diptych Kate envisions herself in *felix culpa*, the *fortunate sin* of self recognition—involving separation, integration, exterior temptation, and self-awareness.

Kate Morgan 2006

This process should not be taken lightly for it involves a soulful inquiry. As evidenced in art-making, the goal is not producing an end product but gaining a deeper awareness of the journey. If our eyes and hearts are open during this journey, then we have a possibility of opening ourselves to the psyche and to the transcendent qualities within an image. To this end, I begin every class with a discussion of the archetypal ways in which each of us sees and perceives. I call this process *finding one's lens*. As Christine Downing reminds us, "symbolic or archetypal thinking is a mode of response *to* the world, which may help free us from entrapment by the illusion of the separation between inner and outer and the disjunction of subject from object."[4]

Our lens is an aggregate of many lenses which are embedded within the individual psyche, resulting in each person's uniquely individual mode of seeing the world we are immersed in. It is a constellation of perspectives we hold that influences: 1) the ways in which we see and perceive; 2) how we interpret what we see; and 3) the manner in which we make judgments and form opinions.

Further, this understanding of lens opens students to a deepened inner relationship with the power and passion of story within the cultural meta-story, to the inner story/image that each individual has. Thus, teaching students to see entails a process of students seeing their own psychic reflections. As a useful analogy from the beginnings of photography, the first practical photographic image-making process was called the daguerreotype (after its inventor, Louis-Jacques-Mandé Daguerre). This process projected the delicate image, formed by the action of light, upon a polished mirror-like surface. This first process simultaneously exhibited itself as a negative and as a positive image to the viewer. The trick to making it appear as a positive was to hold the daguerreotype so that one's own reflected image meshed with the photographic image. The daguerreotype was a mystery and a revelation, even an illusion compelled by the actions of the self. In 1839 it was termed both a "window on the world, and a mirror to the self"; shortly thereafter it was called "a mirror with a memory."

A similar mirror with a memory awareness ignites within students when they begin to tell their stories and to perceive their lenses: namely, how they are the same and yet different from their classmates. As they begin the process, they often believe they are viewing reality; however, they come to understand that the image is also a mirror of themselves. Thus, the image maps the formative territory that is both inner and outer, experience translated into material form. When students see the fuller dimensions of image-making, they also see themselves as journeyers with the fundamental quest of exploring the ways in which they fit into the puzzle of life. It is important that their story is witnessed, first by themselves and then by others. Their story matters; it involves *seeing* their psychic selves within their own images and having the courage to allow their self-image to be seen by others. I have found that students soon realize that each image is in fact a retelling of their story–a mirror with a memory.

Aaron Geiser 2005

The Image at the Center of One's Soul

How can anyone meet us, really know us, until we begin to know ourselves? How can we know ourselves and trust our vision without our full emergence in image? Do we not all seek to find that word or, more precisely, that *image* at the center of our souls? It is the image "which has lain at the center of one's soul" that I believe as teachers of the arts and humanities we must try to bring to the surface. Then we can assist students in discovering ways in which they might dive into their own depths to see anew.

Image involves students seeing through their lenses formed by the memory/remembrance of their own story. Finally, image *is* psyche. As a teacher I understand that students must find their own self-image in order to witness or be able to truly *see* other images. Thus, students cannot truly understand *image* until they have dealt with self-image. Once *envisioned* within the self, students are able to *see* images in entirely new ways. They also gain a fundamental capacity to see and hear the emergent stories that their unique view of images reveals to them and about them. Image is thus a dynamic relationship that is multivalent and available to all. It is this often-overlooked psychic image that I attempt to evoke in the classroom. Indeed, with reference to inner archetypal forces, *how can they meet us face to face till we have faces?*[5]

Notes

[1] C. S. Lewis, *Till We Have Faces* (New York: Harvest Books, 1980), 294.

[2] Dove Corporation, "Evolution," http://www.campaignforrealbeauty.com/flat4.asp?id=6909 (accessed October 19, 2005).

[3] YouTube.com, "Michael Jackson: Transformation from Black to White," http://www.youtube.com/watch?v=9iZdsJQAIQo (accessed October 19, 2005).

[4] Christine Downing, *Mirrors of the Self: Archetypal Images That Shape Your Life* (Los Angeles: Jeremy Tarcher, 1991), xiv.

[5] C. S. Lewis, *Till We Have Faces.*

TEACHING THINKING

Edward S. Casey

No ideas but in the thing itself.
~William Carlos Williams

I

There is a perpetual fascination among educators with finding the right—the most effective—teaching technique. The fascination is already evident in the ancient Greek Sophists' concern with winning arguments at any cost, including whether or not they are true. When Socrates stopped the leading Sophists of his day, such as Protagoras or Gorgias, dead in their tracks, he was in effect challenging the primacy of technique in teaching people how to think. Socrates showed that the technique of seeming to offer a persuasive argument, one with surface plausibility or one not easy to refute, masked a notable lack of *thinking*—really thinking, not just appearing to think or not simply trumping the other in debate. But what is thinking, and how can it be taught? These are my concerns in this brief essay. I speak as a philosopher and a teacher for whom doing philosophy and teaching the subject are indissociable activities.

Teaching Techniques/Teaching Technics. In the era of representation that spells the essence of Western modernity (such is Heidegger's claim), it is not surprising that a preoccupation with technique and technics has arisen in virtually every field, including pedagogy. This preoccupation reflects a twofold commitment to (a) *efficient means,* those designed to accomplish a determinate goal with the greatest speed and the least waste of resources; (b) *scientism,* that is, the idea that modern natural science delivers the ultimate truth about any given subject matter. These two *teloi* are closely yoked, since they share the common conviction that the circumambient world is composed of altogether definite *objects* that are subject to exhaustive description and classification: for example, the human body regarded as the determinate object of medical science. Husserl called this conviction the "natural attitude," that is to say, the assumption that the world is populated by things that are "simply there" (*einfach da*), distributed in space and time and available to complete scientific explanation. In the case of medicine, this is to regard the lived body, that of first-person experience, as nothing but another object—very complex, admittedly, yet still amenable to scientific understanding: if not right now, then certainly someday, with sufficient progress. This latter is supported by technical advances, e.g., MRI scans in the case of the brain.

This tale is not only familiar but itself a symptom of the malady of modernism—an illness that is not medical but a matter of the blockage of thought. Medical techniques such as MRIs do give access to the operations of the cortex and in fine detail, but do they tell us anything significant about what these operations are, regarded as operations *of thought*? Can we honestly say that the enhanced instrumentation at stake in a brain scan conveys anything we didn't already know in our own experience of thinking? Take, for instance, the fact that (as Hobbes put it) "thought is quick." Just *how quick* can, it is true, be determined by a scanning technique. Such a technique can also give us the location of the neural event that is presumed to coincide with the act of thought itself: its "simple location," in Whitehead's term for the appetite of modern science to find and fix the exact locus of any object or event. The cartographic consciousness, also endemic to the modernist mind, sets forth such simple locations on a consistent representational surface—e.g., a brain scan considered as a "map" of the brain. All this requires sophisticated technological means, and it is part of the persuasive force of modern science, epitomized in neurology, that it has so often succeeded in the enterprise of precise representation of brain activity.

But we must ask of this same enterprise: just *what* is being represented? Doubtless a brain event; but what of its content—what of the character or quality of the thought (or memory, or imagination)—of *the very thought that I am myself thinking at this moment?* Can it set that forth? Certainly not in its own terms, and Socrates, were he present today, would be just as skeptical. His insistent question in the dialogues recorded (or devised) by Plato is: *Ti esti?*—that is, "What is X?" "What is the essence of something?" This basic question is prior to other questions such as "Where is X?" "How does X happen?" And it is even prior to "Why X?"

When we live under the domination of technique (as most of us do today), we program ourselves to ask the Where and the How questions to the neglect of the What and the Why ones. Techniques, especially scientific techniques, are means designed to answer where something is and how it happens. Technics are the material instruments upon which techniques themselves rely and by which they are realized. Techniques, however, are modes of effective practice, and they are served and supported by particular technics.

II

In the case of teaching today, technics include PowerPoint presentations, various forms of distance learning, tape recording, typing notes from a lecture into a computer, even video recording. These various technics, and doubtless still others now being devised, are held to improve teaching technique. One calls for the other in a tight technological circle: better technics supports better technique; more efficient technique calls for better technics. But we can ask: should we step straight into this circle? Should we presume that it captures what is essential to teaching? I think not. Let me spell out why I am so skeptical.

There is a place for efficient technique and associated technics— for example, in teaching assessments that form part of an institutional study that is third-person in character from beginning to end. Or perhaps we should say that there is a level for the proper pursuit of the technologically-mediated. But this level is not the level of teaching itself, and it is certainly not that of teaching people how to think or to think better, which is my primary concern as a philosopher who now also teaches depth psychology.

What, then, is teaching thinking? To ask this is really to ask two questions: What is teaching? What is thinking? I shall now offer my take on these difficult, but essential, matters, hoping that this may clarify what teaching is for others who are not philosophers by training but who, nevertheless, are also teaching thinking, whether this is a conscious objective or not. In short, I want to move to a level more basic than that of technique and the technical, one that may make use of these latter but that has its own course of action and criterion of excellence: its own praxis and its own characteristic virtue.

III

To start with: what is thinking? It is not just a cognitive act, nor is it a purely conceptual activity, where "cognition" and "concept" both take for granted the primacy of the intellect over other faculties and powers. Kant's model of cognition (he calls it "experience": *Erfahrung*), for example, is the subsumption of sensory intuitions under preexisting categories, of which there are supposedly only twelve. The result is a "judgment of experience." But experience is not only cognitive, nor is it bound to a set of established concepts or categories. It need not end in determinate judgments (as Kant himself admitted in the case of art). Through experience considered as an active undergoing, we discover new ideas—new ways of thinking. And these ways are not always conceptual in character or judgmental in form; sometimes they are bodily or imagistic, or collective, as in ritualistic actions.

Let us say that thinking is *a transition of mind or psyche from one idea or image to another.* This transition does not merely repeat the initial image or idea but *transforms* it: gives it a new shape and direction as well as a significantly changed content. Or else it changes the kind or level of consideration. It is not subsumptive (as Kant insisted) but outgoing (as the "ex-" of "experience" implies): it goes out to meet novel challenges and directions. In thinking, we experience mental or psychical transformations, where this does not mean merely submitting to them as givens but rather actively undertaking them ourselves, making them our own, taking responsibility for them. The transition of thinking is a movement we make ourselves—and only by ourselves. It is this movement that teaching, in my view, should foster.

Before coming more fully to teaching itself, let me distinguish between eight modes of thinking, four of which are creative and four deficient in one way or another. Each of these modalizes thinking and shows that it is not just one kind of activity but always potentially many.

A. First, then, the positive modalities of thinking:
  (i) *thinking of* (or on, at): this is the direct seizing of ideas or images by making them more evident, salient, or pertinent in

our ongoing lives; when I think of X, I put myself in the very presence of X, at its doorstep as it were—as we imply when we say "Think of it!";

(ii) *thinking through:* staying with a theme or topic (both being kinds of content) and exploring its inner nisus, that toward which it tends;

(iii) *thinking out:* following out an idea or image to its limit, and glimpsing what is just beyond; this often occurs stepwise, as when we think out the consequences of a contemplated action; it always involves a certain range or scope;

(iv) *thinking over:* this amounts to reviewing content that has already become consolidated or thematic, hovering over it, as it were; it is not necessarily perfunctory, since we can discover new or neglected aspects of the idea or image we are thinking over.

B. Regarding deficient modalities:

(i) *thinking around:* instead of thinking our thought, i.e., staying with its own content, we may move around it, going into its vicinity or margin, not to discover something new but to dwell there evasively;

(ii) *thinking alongside:* rather than focusing on a theme or topic, we can turn to something juxtaposed with it—its "paired associate," in William James's term: e.g., instead of thinking of William the philosopher-psychologist, I think of his brother Henry the novelist;

(iii) *thinking away:* this is diversionary thinking, failing to think of, out, through or over it; this can be done impulsively or deliberately; either way, it comes down to *not thinking* what is to be thought, refusing to enter into its demands;

(iv) *thinking-on-the-occasion:* such thinking is the creature of its occasion, "situational thinking," as we can call it; it possesses no force or vector of its own; it goes nowhere that is not dictated by the very circumstance in which it arises.

I set forth this brief conspectus of modes of thought not to be definitive or fully conspectus of ways in which we think but to suggest that human thinking occurs in many forms, not one (or two) only. It is a matter of what I like to call "the multiplicity of the mental" or, more adequately expressed, "the polyvalence of the psychical." In each case, thinking occurs by a traverse motion *across* an ideational or imagistic domain: not just *from* one idea or image *to* another (strictly regarded, this would come to just thinking alongside) but in a lateral move that sweeps through the in-between space in such a way as to constitute that space itself. It is not a matter of moving through a preconstituted spatial spread or stretch, as when we speak of a "trajectory" that is imposed on a neutral field or ground, but of a *spatializing* motion that is the act of thinking itself. In such *spatializing*, a sense of agency is indispensable: I must be able to recognize that this transformative action is one I am myself performing and not one I am merely borrowing or imitating. It is my own thinking, though not as implying that it belongs to myself alone; it can be shared with others, as when it excites their thinking in turn. I am responsible for the thinking I do—both for the act itself and for its consequences—and teaching inculcates this very sense of responsibility.

IV

Teaching, then, has the primary task of instilling a sense of agency in the person learning. It aims not just at getting people to think in one or more of the four positive modalities I have singled out above, but at inculcating the conviction that it is *their own* thinking that is occurring—that they are having "their own thoughts" and not just re-enacting those of others.

It is tempting to transfer the teacher's thinking into the mind or psyche of the learner. That way lies rote learning: learning by imitation, repetition, or substitution. This is the kind of learning that colludes so easily with techniques and technics, as I have described them in Section I above. In each case, there is the fundamental fallacy that teaching and learning are a matter of *communication*—that is, the transmission of a definite message from one person (or group of persons) to another. The assumption is that there is a determinate content that is manifested in the communication, and that the teacher's job is to pass on this content, unchanged, to the learner who, in turn, is nothing but a receptacle for this same content, a passive *tabula rasa*. The only responsibility at stake in learning on this delimited model is that of being uncritically absorptive for the messages sent by the teacher and, increasingly in recent times, reliant upon the facilities of technique or the materialities of technologically-mediated machines.

The character of teaching is very different when it is conceived as a process of *expression* rather than of communication. In expressive discourse or imagining, there is a continual change in the content as it moves from the expressive person to those who take it in. No single or same message is conveyed; here, as in poetry, it is a "heresy of paraphrase" to formulate in so many words what is being expressed. As Merleau-Ponty puts it, the word (action, act, performance) is not just "spoken" but is itself "speaking": it is a matter of *la parole parlante*, the word that speaks. We can understand this as saying: *the thought that thinks,* the thought that does not merely rethink but *thinks for itself.*

But once more this does not mean only to think alone, *solus ipse,* without the assistance of others. Each thinking person—which is to say, each learner—is bound in an expressive matrix with a teacher. This teacher need not be an institutionally- sanctioned instructor; he or she can be an informal mentor, a friend who challenges one to think anew, or even a part of oneself that, by prior internalization, acts as a teacher within (as when we call upon ourselves to surpass previous acts of learning). Further, "the teacher" can equally well be an entire community: one's elders, peers, neighbors. Ultimately, learning always takes place in some significant community, whether this is institutional (e.g., a college, university, or school) or informal (as when citizens meeting by chance on a street corner think out what steps a particular political action might take). This educational community can also be memorial or imaginal in character—as when learners belong to a tradition of learning or imagine what such a tradition might be like.

Nor does teaching/learning have to happen in spoken words or by printed texts. It can also transpire in images: this is why I have been insisting on the coeval status of images or words in the generation of thinking. Teachers of painting or dance or photography help others to think in highly imagistic media—and I mean *think* in the various valorized senses I sketched in the last section. For I can think of things in imagistic formats as well as in terms of ideational content; I can think them through, think them out, and think them over—all in images. Where images are presentational in character, thrusting themselves forward for our cognizance, ideas are characteristically schematic. One is a matter mainly of display, the other of compressed or withheld presence: where images come forward to us, ideas are experienced as already in the process of withdrawing.

Images are multiple in character: not just visual but auditory, tactile, kinesthetic, So too are the ideas at stake in nonimagistic thinking: some are discrete and isolated, some are deeply connected to other ideas and complexes of ideas. In instances, the theme of multiplicity resonates throughout. This is all the more the case insofar as ideas and images can be combined, and often are so: e.g., in the number forms that Francis Galton showed to obtain in many people's idea of a series of numbers (say, the numbers 1 to 20 as these form various sinuous shapes in one's mind). If multiplicity obtains so broadly in the domain of ideas and images, it follows that ways of teaching must be themselves intrinsically multiple. There can be no one correct way of teaching thinking if the very content of thinking itself is polyadic. This is not to say, however, that every kind of teaching is equally valid—that it is a matter of indifference as to how one teaches, that anything goes. My point is rather that teaching that matters should always be the teaching of thinking: yet, given the multiplicity of the two basic media of thinking, ideas and images (and their respective varieties), there are many ways to teach people how to think: how to think broadly and well, in a forceful as well as in a nuanced manner.

V

My theme has been "teaching thinking." This phrase juxtaposes two active participles. When we attend to this grammatical form, it implies that teaching is not the teaching of *thoughts*: it is not the inculcation of already-thought thoughts but thoughts *in the making* (to add a third participle). Teaching that works—that has a significant effect on learning how to think—encourages the learner to enter the edge of the last thought. For the ultimate aim is to teach thinking in the act of thinking. From this it ensues that the onus is on the teacher to think him- or herself—to exemplify the act of thinking by modeling it for the learner. This modeling is not to be reduced to a mere technique for teaching thinking—as if there were a certain number of required steps to pursue in coming to think on one's own. However tempting it may be, such a technique betrays the pluralist principle on which I have been insisting. What the teacher owes the student is to embody the activity of thinking itself: in her words, her gestures, her attitude toward being in the classroom, or his ways of treating students in that setting. Thus the effort is not to exemplify *pure* thinking, thinking *qua* thinking: this latter belongs to formal and informal logic (or to God who, according to Aristotle, is to be defined as *nous noein*: pure mind thinking itself). The true teacher, the teacher who *matters*, is neither a pure logician nor a god. Indeed, to teach logic itself well is not to teach a set of infallible methods. It is to show one's students what it means to think consequentially, cogently, clearly, and plausibly. (Or, if it is to teach methods, this is only when "method" is understood in its original sense as a way to proceed validly—recalling that the *hodos* of *methodos* signifies "way.")

If (as is often said in the wake of Socrates), teaching is "midwifery" (*maieusis*), then it is not assisting the birth of fully formed thoughts but of the process of thinking itself. Such teaching ushers into existence ideas or images that are genuinely *embryonic*—that are at the first stage of becoming rather than representing an intact being such as a full-term baby. It is to bring the infant in each learner alive, where "infant" stays true to its original sense of "not-yet-speaking" (from *in-fans*). However, the infant does *think*: he thinks in and through his nascent perception and orientation, touching and hearing. In such primal thinking—semiotic if not yet fully symbolic—the infant is on his way to words. The teacher is a midwife to the embryonic infant in the learner, assisting the rebirth of thinking, this time in language, giving the learner a second chance to begin to think: to think anew, to think creatively, to think differently than he has been taught institutionally heretofore.

Teaching, taking place in already existing words ("spoken speech"), inculcates a revived thinking process in the form of genuinely "speaking speech." The teacher tries to elicit yet unsaid words that will articulate newly emerging thoughts: the words that are the expressive vehicles of the thoughts. (Or else, in the case of the nonliterary arts: the images that express thoughts in a nonverbal medium.) He or she demonstrates ways of thinking in word or image: new ways of thinking, prior to, but necessary for, new ways of acting and knowing.

VI

The genuine teacher is at once exemplary and expressive—exemplary of what it is to think and expressive of how it feels to think. In short, she or he is exemplary of *the experience of thinking*, that is to say, of thinking on one's feet, thinking spontaneously: *thinking in one's own person*. This last point is crucial. Thinking in first-person is precisely what a sheer technique of thinking (much less a mere technic) cannot

141

achieve on its own: in a technique or a technic, there is no person there—no person thinking who stands before the learner as actually engaged in thinking. Such engagement, properly performed, is at once felicitous and infectious. It is done with finesse (and not just skill) and in such a way as to call for emulation on the part of those who witness it. It is self-enacted on the part of the teacher—seemingly effortless (even if requiring a lifetime of practice)—and self-engendering on the part of the learner, who must make every effort in the present to begin to learn how to think (now and for the nth time).

What the learner must learn is not only how to think—though this is the main task—but *to dare to think*. Kant, in his celebrated essay on the Enlightenment, said that its primary lesson was "to dare to know" (*sapere aude*); but before knowing there is thinking, which has its own daring. The learner must dare to think as he or she has never thought before. Everything else is inauthentic repetition, comparable to plagiarizing texts posted on the web. There is an authentic repetition that consists in "recollecting forwards" (in Kierkegaard's apt phrase). We can take this to mean that on the basis of the teacher's exemplary act of thinking outright, the learner dares to carry forward into his or her own life a comparably bold practice of thinking: thinking in ever different situations, each of which calls for thinking in continually new ways. This signifies a willingness to *think otherwise* than established habits of thinking permit—such habits amounting to little more than commonly held beliefs or opinions (*doxai*, in Plato's word for these latter).

By the same token, however, the teacher, if he or she is to live in accordance with what (or, rather, how) he or she teaches, also has to continue to dare to think differently—not only in the classroom but in every room, and outside the room as well: in one's circle of family and friends, as a citizen, on the streets, in the nation, internationally, everywhere. Just as nothing more is required to be a true thinker, so nothing less will do. This is why Socrates is still today the exemplary thinker of the West: he dared to think outwardly (often outrageously!) not just with his pupils and disciples but everywhere in Athens—all over the agora. We who teach would do well to emulate his example in our teaching as in our lives. Are we up to this task? If not yet (and who is?), can we at least dare to commence it?

•   •   •   •   •

"No ideas but in the thing itself." Just so: the poet is surely right. But we need to modulate these words of Williams: no ideas but in the activity of thinking itself. Otherwise said, the "thing itself" is the act of thinking, whether this happens in poetic language, bodily gestures, the creation of images, or the thinking of ideas themselves. Teachers and learners alike need to heed this line of thought. They need to put it into practice—into every practice they undertake—and to pursue it in every experience they undergo. Such is the task, such the challenge: to think anew, in each and every disparate circumstance.

Teaching is teaching thinking—ways of thinking, in image or idea, that exemplify the thinking expressed and enacted in the very practice (not the technique or technics) of teaching itself. In the end, as in the beginning, this is what teaching calls teachers such as ourselves to do—day in and week out, in the classroom and beyond.

THE EROS OF TEACHING

Christine Downing

When I was in high school my best friend was Anne Martin. Anne was the only other scholarship student in our small class at one of northern New Jersey's fancy private schools for girls. I'd been there since fifth grade; she came in ninth grade. I was almost surely the first even-remotely Jewish student ever to attend the school, she probably the first Catholic. But what really set us apart from our classmates and drew us to one another was how much we both loved books: reading them and talking about them. I remember how that first year we read all of Jane Austen together, book by book, and how the next year it was George Eliot. But I also remember how disappointed I was when I told her of my ongoing love for Jo March and she let me know that Louisa May Alcott was not a good writer, not worth spending one's time on. She said this with great authority; her father was an English Literature professor.

Now that I have begun remembering Anne, I need to go on. We spent so much time together all through high school, especially on weekends. Of course, we had differing interests, too. In one of our art classes, she discovered that she loved working with clay. I still remember the amazingly perfect copy she made of the famous Nefertiti head and the months she had spent working on it. I loved playing hockey, basketball, and lacrosse, pursuits that bored her. Perhaps another telling clue: for our senior theses she wrote on Emily Dickinson, I on Dostoevski. When it came time to go to college, she went to Vassar where all the best students from our school had always gone; I chose a coeducational school, Swarthmore. She majored in sculpture, I in literature. I got married at the end of my junior year; she became more and more devoted to her art. We drifted apart but never quite lost touch. She won a Prix de Rome and went to Italy and a year or two later killed herself—I think because she had discovered that though she was indeed gifted, indeed *good,* she was never going to be great.

What led me to think of Anne was trying to explain my appreciation of May Sarton's *A Small Room.*[1] It is so clearly *not* a great book—the characters are not fully realized, the plot is a bit contrived, the language never sings, the metaphors are too obvious, the resolution too pat. I am even prepared to call it a small book—and yet I am moved by it, moved by it to reflect on my own experience as a teacher in a way that no other academic novel has called me to do. Perhaps because it is about *teaching* and *about love—not* about adultery (as fiction set in the academy so often turns out to be) but about the love of teaching.

I find myself wondering what it would have been like to have read this novel about Lucy Winter's initiation into the world of teaching when it first came out twenty years ago, just before I began my own academic career. I am conscious even now of reading with a double perspective. Of course, I read it from my own present standpoint, that of a fairly seasoned professor just over fifty, that is, of someone just about Sarton's age when she wrote the book. But I also find myself identifying with twenty-seven-year-old Lucy Winter and her fascination with Carryl Cope, the fiftyish professor who serves as her initiator and "makes her fall in love with a profession." Strange sometimes how a book falls into our hands just when we are ready for *it*—just before beginning this one I had found myself engaged in a powerful inner dialogue between just these two selves, my twenty-seven-year-old self and the me of now.

My hunch is that when we academics read novels set in a college or university, we will amplify what is actually given in the text with our own experience. And a novel about initiation will recall us to our own beginnings—to our perhaps almost-romantic sense of vocation, to the inevitably naive and innocent dreams and hopes that we brought to our first jobs—and to the vital fears, self-doubts, conflicts, confusions, and failures that were also present (and that we have gradually learned we never fully leave behind). A novel like this gives us an opportunity to step outside for a moment and to see this world freshly. At her first faculty party, Lucy is told that she and the other newly hired faculty are in the position of anthropologists confronting a strange tribe. And throughout the novel Lucy remains a little outside—and thus is entrusted with confidences from all the major players in the story that unfolds. She seems able to see more wholly than she will ever see again, once she becomes an insider with a clearly defined role of her own.

The language of initiation pervades the novel. It opens with a train ride that marks Lucy's separation from her earlier world. She has recently lost a beloved but emotionally distant father and has just broken an engagement to a male lover; she is on her way to her first teaching assignment at a small prestigious women's college. It feels to her that she might be entering upon a "novitiate"; she wonders whether she is on her way to finding her true vocation. The entire novel takes place during her first fall semester; it begins and ends with a faculty party in a "small room" at the home of one of the established professors. At the first such gathering there is much talk of the school being a world set apart, like a mystery cult or secret society. Lucy feels that everyone seems to be wearing masks and talking a different language. She is pointedly asked, "Is this just an interlude for you?"

Lucy herself isn't clear; she knows that she has just stumbled into this world. As she confides that she had only gone to graduate school at Harvard so as to be near her fiancé while he was in medical school, that she had never really thought beyond that, I remember how I, too, really made my way into teaching only by accident. I had so loved being in graduate school in the midst of others who enjoyed thinking seriously and talking passionately about the things that interested me most; it was only as I completed my course work that I realized the only way to stay in such a world was to move from being a student to becoming a teacher. For me as for Lucy (and I suspect for many of us), it is teaching itself that teaches us to love it.

Though the fictional Appleton is a women's college, it is not quite an all-women's world. There are a few male faculty, and they have wives. But the focus really falls on the interactions among the women faculty—none of whom are married or have children—and between them and their female students. My own first twelve years of teaching were spent at a women's college—larger than this one and more closely connected to a male counterpart—but I recognize the scene. At my institution, there were also very few married female

147

professors, and I remember well what an anomaly I with my five children represented. In the novel there are two middle-aged women who've been together for twenty years and whom everyone recognizes as a couple—as was true at just about every women's college of that era. I also recognize the intensity of the connections between female faculty and students that never become explicitly erotic (as it did in my experience by the end of the decade). Because students enter this novel only as the faculty come to know them, there is no hint of the quasi-lesbian intensities of their involvements with one another that I remember so clearly. However, even during her interview for the job, Lucy is emphatically told: "We are not interested in producing marriageable young ladies" but rather in nurturing our students' intellects and fostering excellence.

In the book about the Greek goddesses I published a year ago, I wrote about the powerful role Athene represents and how she has played out in my life—a role she plays in this novel as well. (I think I am right in remembering that she is the only goddess invoked.) We are shown how much Athene can *give* women—a blessing of their intellectual gifts, their creativity, their courage—but also of the costs of devotion to her. Like Athene, all the major figures in the novel are father's daughters; all seem to carry a deep father wound (whereas there are almost no references to mothers).

There are several wonderful classroom scenes, including one account of an experienced teacher's subtle guidance of a seminar that evokes awe in Lucy—and, I must admit, in me. The report of Lucy's own very first upper-division class serves to introduce the central theme of the novel—the place of *eros* in the relation between faculty and student. Lucy spends that first hour talking very personally about herself, about her relation to her father and to the important teachers (all male) who inspired her own love of literature—and is then dismayed when after class a student tries to share with her how devastated she remains by the recent death of her father. "You're confusing me with an imaginary someone, a father confessor or friend," she tells her; "I won't be that." Yet Lucy is appalled by the cruelty of her rejection and hastens to consult Hallie Summerson, the older teacher whom she already views as a mentor. "I don't believe in personal relationships between teachers and students, do you?" she asks. "Theoretically, no," Hallie somewhat ambiguously replies. The novel explores this topic in a rich, complex way that serves to underline my own sense of how hard—impossible, perhaps—it is to find the right balance. Later, Carryl Cope will tell Lucy, "The relation between student and teacher must be about the most complex and ill-defined there is." Lucy comes to sense how difficult it will always be to know when to withdraw, when to yield or approach; she comes to appreciate that such relationships are "as various, *as* unpredictable, as a love affair." Hallie affirms that "what we give our students, whether we are personal with them or not, is the marrow, the essence of ourselves, what true lovers ask of love."

Later, Carryl helps her see that one cannot just evade or eliminate the transferences that are inevitably invoked, not only the transferences that students project on their teachers but also those projected by teachers on students. Carryl recognizes that her own favorite student, Jane Seaman, has transferred longings for recognition from her father onto her—but also that she has seen herself in Jane, sought to give the student what she had once hoped for herself. Carryl also tries to help Lucy understand, "We couldn't do this without all of who we are—without our personal lives, our passions, our conflicts."

Throughout the novel Lucy wonders what it is that she is really trying to teach—whether content, knowledge, or how to live. She does so in a way that leads me to wonder about this for myself. My (tentative) answer is that I want to communicate my love—not exactly of my students, though not exactly *not* of my students—but more explicitly my love of the books, the authors, the ways of looking at the world that have moved and inspired me, and my love of the process of inquiry that brought me to those books, those writers; I want to encourage my students to find what might move them in the same way—and come to love looking for it. In the novel Carryl is clear she wants to teach her students to *think*—but I guess I want to encourage them to *love*—and yet I sense that we are not as far apart as this formulation might suggest, for I would wish they might come to love thinking and to discover that one can think with one's whole being!

The plot of the novel revolves around an exceptionally brilliant student, Jane Seaman, who was mentioned at that initial party as a protégé of Carryl Cope. Almost by accident, Lucy shortly discovers that Jane has plagiarized an at-that-time little-known essay on the *Iliad* *by* Simone Weil; Jane's only slightly paraphrased version is being published as the lead article in a publication of Appleton student essays. Lucy—and later everyone else—is puzzled by why such an unquestionably gifted student would do something so incredibly risky and stupid. As the story unfolds we learn that Jane herself believes she has done it in order to be found out, in order to free herself from what has become an unbearable pressure to excel. Initially, she responded with great joy to the encouragement Carryl Cope had given her but then felt that the bar kept being raised higher and higher; the pressure had become too great. Jane essentially ends up having a nervous breakdown, which forces Carryl to come to terms with the limitations of her blindness to anything about Jane other than her intellectual gifts. Carryl comes to accept responsibility both for expecting too much from Jane and for not having given her the more personal attention she really longed for. "I wasn't there," she says (though the novel encourages us to trust Carryl's lesbian partner's insistence that Carryl really loved Jane).

At the December party that completes Lucy's initiation, almost everyone present tries to make sense of the crisis into which this episode has plunged the whole college. One of her male colleagues stammeringly protests, "C-C-Carryl, it's very noble of you, and all that, to feel responsible for Jane, but I doubt actually if it would have been such a very great help if you had given whatever it was you think you withheld." Lucy recognizes that perhaps there is no generalizable lesson to be drawn.

What I take away from the novel is a reminder that (like Carryl—but in our own ways) we *will* fail, will get it wrong, will do damage sometimes (and I'm reminded of damage I've done)—but also that the opportunity being a teacher offers us to share what we love and to encourage others to find what they can love is an incomparable gift.

Notes

[1] May Sarton, *The Small Room* (New York: Norton, 1961).

THE AUTHORITY OF THE TEACHER

Claudia Allums

In one way or another, I realize now, the classroom has always been my psychic home. At the same time, although I do not have bad memories about teachers or school and some of my *best* childhood memories come from experiences with teachers, I do not recall enjoying *being* in school as much as I enjoyed other childhood activities, like playing in the neighbor's sandbox or building forts in our backyard. This attitude is typical, I know. But the *act* of teaching was always an important part of how I viewed myself, and *that* was with me from my earliest memories. After my first unpleasant days in prekindergarten, I loved teachers and respected them, as a whole, more than any other group of adults in my life. I can recall summers when at eight and nine years of age I marshaled good-natured (obviously) neighborhood peers into submitting to my classroom antics: story time and craft time stand out in my memory as my most effective teaching venues.

My desire to inform and lead was a heady passion. It appears I felt some kind of personal insult at others' ignorance about things that I deemed important and, more so, that I considered my awareness of this lack as a license to instruct. Of course, my own ignorance about things must have been secondary to theirs because I recall that my personal goal was not so much to learn and grow myself but to correct this sad state in others. I approached teaching in an attitude of arrogance, I'm afraid, with a sense that I knew not only the questions but also the answers and so had a right to stand before others and direct them. The best thing I can say about my mindset in those early years is that my lack of concern for how my genial peers felt about

151

their mandatory summer schooling suggests I had the makings of someone able to withstand the broad range of insults—from apathy to antagonism—that one endures at the hands of youth whenever one stands before them in a classroom.

For good or ill, my years in college taught me little about teaching or other matters, and so I took my first position as a high school teacher a bit older and with a bit more information but much the same as I had been before. With this first teaching position, though, I felt a delight I had never known. Others would pay me, modestly, to do what I had been volunteering to do all my life; they would pay me to *be* what I had *been* for as long as I could remember. It was like being paid for breathing. I had an official grade book and a contract. I was a teacher!

In those first years, my classroom was my life. I spent nearly all of my time preparing for or taking care of my lesson plans, my room, and my students. Had the small, religious institution where I was employed been more of a school and less of a refuge for people fleeing the iniquities of the world, I might have learned more about my intellectual responsibilities and the personal habits of a teacher. But I was one of two teachers in the high school English department, and although the junior, I found myself to be the more serious and dedicated one. And so my burning desire (and need) to have a teaching mentor, to work under the wings, if you will, of one wiser and more dedicated than I, would not be realized there. I knew that I lacked wisdom and expertise and needed guidance in spite of my enthusiasm, but I had no one to point me in the right direction. Moreover, I am sorry to see that, as a whole, we still do not consider it imperative to mentor and nurture young teachers in our schools in meaningful ways, such that so many young teachers suffer the same fate that I did.

What I did, at that time, was pour heart and mind into my work as best I could. I spent hours tending to my physical classroom: with posters and what I hoped were inspirational graphics I tried to impress on my students an image of the big world outside of their own adolescent experience. I spent my weekends constructing elaborate lesson plans for the following week and drafting worksheets and other enticements to pique students' grammatical curiosity. I spent countless hours with them outside of class, listening to their triumphs and failures while always empathic to their concerns. It was a wonderful, exhausting experience that I wouldn't trade for the world. Although I am certain that these students could have learned much more from hands more sure than mine, I am relieved that many of them have initiated and maintained contact with me over the years, suggesting to me that our time together was meaningful if not useful. I am now content to allow that both they and I enjoyed some lasting benefits from our mutual journey.

After teaching in this fashion for nearly ten years—passionately, but without what I later discovered to be a clear sense of purpose—I found myself in a completely unfamiliar and dispiriting state. I lost the joy of my work. I was questioning the one thing in my life that I had always known for a certainty: I was a teacher. I had always wanted to be the best possible teacher and always tried to guide young lives toward noble aspirations. As a person of faith, I also felt a responsibility to an eternal action higher than merely human ends and means. By many standards I was a success. I was often able to communicate the factual content of my lessons to even the most unreachable students and leave them with more information than was in their possession when first we met. I was employing as many pedagogical skills as I could, and I developed the habit of pressing myself to go deeper into my discipline, to know my content and the varied means to express the truths about human experience that I knew existed in great poetry. But in spite of this, I was increasingly restless about the integrity of what I was doing.

In the spring of 1989, while serving as an assistant principal, I sat across the desk from a teacher with whom I had requested an audience so that he could explain his high school humanities program to me. As I sat with this wise, kind teacher —I quickly realized, *here* was the mentor for whom I had longed!—something in my teacherly soul began to awaken. Now my friend, Dr. Daniel Russ must have seen the desperation lurking behind the professional courtesy in my eyes because not long into our conversation, he began to talk to me about a program he knew, one that had been created to renew teachers in spirit and in mind. I do not remember what else I learned about his school at that time (although I would later be privileged to teach there and even to lead this very department), but by the end of this meeting, I was convinced that I must attend the Summer Institute for Teachers at The Dallas Institute of Humanities and Culture that very year. It felt like my life depended on it.

I was reborn that summer at The Dallas Institute. Here, for the first time in my life, was gathered a group of like-minded people who thought as highly of teachers and of the profession as I did. Here, for the first time in my life, I saw a true community of thinkers. Inspired by the vision and spirit of one extraordinary teacher, Dr. Louise Cowan, my professors there acted with the gently communal yet rigorous spirit I had always imagined should be the way that those with the most education should conduct themselves. At every turn, we school teachers were treated as professionals, and this by some of the brightest college professors I had ever known. The whole atmosphere of the class was collegial yet intellectually challenging.

We were honored first because we were teachers, but our professors' respect for us inspired us to respond to the work with our best efforts. All of this was done in a spirit of generosity and rigor that I had never experienced before. *This is what it feels like to be in a real classroom,* I remember thinking after the first hour of the class. If I had not learned anything other than this graceful and intelligent code of manners, this awareness alone would have exceeded the value of any other educational experience I had ever had. But what I discerned as the animating force *behind* the spirit of this amazing community is what changed my life and work, because this larger action, as Aristotle might call it, the action out of which this astonishing community was born and sustained, is what led me to understand the true authority of the teacher.

Simply stated, what I began to learn that summer was the classical concept of *form,* the form of my discipline, the form of my calling. Form, as we engaged the term that summer, had to do with the Platonic notion that objects and ideas that exist in the physical world are actually manifestations of those things in a perfect, invisible realm of forms. For example, a literal chair in my classroom is a chair and gains its shape, not because it simply *is* and *sits* there, but because it is imitating and participating in the perfect form of "chair" as it exists in the realm of forms. Although the physical construction of a chair varies greatly, there are still, Plato suggested, fundamental qualities that make an object participate in chairness, as we might call it. The same is true of ideas like justice and honor; these are not simply ideas that a given generation invents and enacts; they are ideas that are living manifestations of the *forms* of justice and honor that exist in an immutable, invisible order.

But form was not only important for its origination but also because it provided a way to access the meaning of things. The notion

154

of a realm of forms suggests a world less random and chaotic than our modern sensibilities would have us believe, and it particularly resonated with my hope-filled teacherly soul. Because form means that a thing is not simply a sum of its physical or rational parts, it suggests that it has an essence that cannot be empirically known and measured. Since the 17th century in the West, we have been working against this notion. Our conviction that all things can be fully and rationally understood has caused us to lose a sense of what we often intuit, that a thing is not simply what we can see but is an amalgam of visible and invisible things. Taken in this way, accepting the nature of forms requires one to submit to them, because understanding can only be achieved when one recognizes the immeasurable qualities as well as those things one can rationally perceive.

As a result of this notion that things have their meaning and form according to something outside of what one can know logically, I began to see that teaching is not just something we do because we might be good at it but something we do because meaning exists and deserves our attention. In this wonderful summer class amidst those amazing teachers I grasped that although some of us love to teach, the profession does not gather its meaning from our participation in it. Up to that point, I taught because I loved literature, because I loved teaching, and because I loved my students. I had always known what a privilege it was to do what I loved, but I had confused my passion for my work with that which gave it its meaning. My experience at the Summer Institute began to reveal the inherent form of teaching and learning as something higher than my personal experience of these, to which my students and I must aspire and submit.

That summer of 1989, the bond of the intellectual community was forged in our acceptance of the idea that the meaning we were seeking was larger than all of us and that it had an existence and value beyond even our collective understanding. It humbled us and yet made us proud to be a part of this miraculous profession. Grasping form turned our attention away from ourselves, away from our desire to seek merely bright or even brilliant insights, to strive, instead, for deeper understanding. The idea of forms became a great equalizer because even the brightest among us were engaged in seeking this higher thing instead of in correcting those of us who occupied a lower intellectual terrain. We all learned *submission* that summer—an uncomfortable word for teachers—but arrogance was an absurd response in light of this overwhelming evidence of form existing beyond our highest aspirations. At the same time, since we were consciously moving towards understanding something of such value, our learning experience was rich, vital, and a delight in and for itself.

Afterward, thinking about *teaching* as having a form outside of my experience of it provided me with the internal navigation I had always lacked. I found my authority to teach. When I recognized that even my educated estimation of a thing was not that which gave it meaning, I stopped thinking about knowledge as a tool by which I could achieve mastery and could therefore teach my *students* to achieve this mastery. I know this sounds naïve, but I think this is an intellectual arrogance that is an occupational hazard, as we say, into which teachers can naturally fall, and our attempts to confine teaching solely to measurement and standardization in these last decades has only contributed to our delusion of control over the full meaning of things. This modern supposition that *we make all meaning* is what motivates students to ask the proverbial question: "What does this have to do with the real world?" In addition, I think it is what causes us to respond to students with those unsatisfying and wilting admonitions.

It is important for me to admit that I did not stop testing or insisting on assignments. Nor did I cease teaching grammar and syntax or vocabulary words or how to identify common literary motifs, nor did I stop expecting my students to master concepts and facts. But these objectives became the *first* steps of our intellectual inquiry rather than its end because we accepted that there was something behind them, something higher than our classroom standard, higher than the tests, higher than our department or school. I had to change my expectations—in most cases, I had to increase them—because what we were striving to comprehend was more complicated and more precious than any of us had previously grasped. Class periods became opportunities for important inquiry, and the tools that we used—even what had before seemed the most tedious and mundane facts and devices—became useful when seen in their proper place.

Practically speaking, the mutual respect born of this appreciation of form transformed the relationships in my classes. Much as I had become a junior colleague to my university professors that summer at The Dallas Institute, my high school students and I—from freshmen to seniors—began to see ourselves as on a journey together. They recognized me as a valid guide by merit of my having given myself so passionately to the discipline, and they also witnessed my sometimes-clumsy struggle to understand these things that were even beyond *my* comprehension. I could teach them facts about *Moby-Dick* and point out important themes and poetic constructions, but to communicate a rational understanding of the mystery behind the terror of the white whale, I was not much better prepared than they to articulate this in factual terms. What we did together was to bear witness, in awe, of the profundity of the mysterious collusion between the visible and invisible realms.

Moreover, because I became concerned about things larger than grades and grading systems, I was forced to change my expectations for students' work and assignments. My expectations increased. I was no longer a neurotic eccentric who manufactured worksheets and outlines that took the spirit out of learning while they filled my grade books. I still gave daily quizzes, and we continued having exams, but much of what I taught was more complicated and subtle, based on writing, thought, conversation, and ideas. Because we had raised our sights, it didn't make sense to conduct classes in the standard way. I asked for a high level of maturity from my students, and they responded to all of my expectations. Instead of forcing my schedule on them, I required that they take responsibility for managing their own workload and for letting me know when they could not meet a class-assigned deadline. As a result, my life was no longer a nightmare of petitioning for late or makeup work, and my relationships with my students were no longer strained because of my badgering them about being tardy or about incomplete assignments. Those conditions simply didn't exist anymore.

An additional personal benefit was that with almost no exceptions in those years, students who were habitually asking or allowing their parents to step in and take over when they were in "grade trouble" instead chose to address these difficulties with me themselves. They considered me an ally because they knew that I was seeking higher things, things that we realized were important to all of us. They knew that their grades were not simply arbitrary sums but were, instead, a reflection of how willing they were to invest in their own existence. Further, I was told by more than a few of them, when they failed to complete an assignment or did it poorly, that they considered it a loss. They realized that *they* had broken the trust between us, a trust that had been established for their growth and good. And when I began trusting in my authority as a teacher to guide students toward meaning rather than simply keeping the favor of my young charges, they began to respect me in a way that I had not previously known. At the same time, when I accepted that my primary responsibility to my students was not to be a confidant or peer but rather to be a respectable mentor and guide, I began to have a profound sense of their human experiences that made my former compassion for them seem affected and small.

I don't know whether the joy that I experienced in my last years in the high school classroom could have occurred, to this degree, earlier in my career or whether that success was a blessed convergence of experience and insight. Part of me believes that if, as a young teacher, I had been in possession of the idea of this larger, engendering form that I discovered that summer at the Dallas Institute, I would have made much more sense to my students and would have spent far less time struggling against their adolescent whims. What I do believe now is that even for those of us who feel we have been born to it, for those of us who feel it in our bones, teaching is a profession and not just a personality. We diminish its impact in the world if we make ourselves or our students our object rather than focus on meaning in the world. Meaning is everywhere we look, and we, as teachers, are its guardians in the culture. It's in the various ways we know things, in math and science and history. It's in the literature and philosophy and foreign languages we learn, because these are all ways that we deepen our human experience. Finally, the authority of the teacher, I believe, paradoxically comes in proportion to the degree to which the teacher is willing to open herself—with submission and respect—to the unseen things that give life meaning.

TEACHING JOSEPH CAMPBELL AND THE ARTHURIAN ROMANCE

Evans Lansing Smith

The classroom is a *temenos*, a sacred space of revelation and transformation, where the mysteries of soul-making are undertaken and reflected upon. Teaching embodies the energies of the mind, the heart, and the spirit—the fusion of which enables, and is enabled by, the educational process. As a master of the classroom and lecture hall, Joseph Campbell was fond of pointing out that the word "education" is derived from the Latin *"e-ducere*, 'to lead or draw forth.'"[1] He called this process "hermetic pedagogy," for education is an alchemical opus of transforming base metals into gold. Every class session catalyzes a hero's journey.

My own connection with Joseph Campbell began with a journey, a dream, and a poem. Not knowing what I wanted to do after graduating from Williams College in 1972, I decided to get a degree in Creative Writing from Antioch International, and so went abroad for the first time to spend a year and a half working on a novel and a bunch of poems in London and Dublin. Crossing the Irish Channel, on seas traveled by Tristan and Isolde, I met, fell in love with, and had a powerful dream about the wrong woman at the right time.

I dreamt I was on a large ferry, which struck and cut through a large sea dragon that encircled the ship while leaving the port. The boat then began to spin around, and a whirlpool sucked drowning sailors down into a maelstrom of froth and blood. When I leaned over the ship's railings to try to rescue them, a naked woman emerged from the center of the whirlpool, and I reached down to help her on board the deck. When I ran my hands along her thighs, they were goose-pimpled and scaly. Some of the crew members then took her off to get her dressed. When she came back to me, she was wearing the large glasses of the girl from Maryland I had fallen in love with. She told me the crew had committed her to a mental asylum.

During the months that followed, I wrote a poem about the dream and called it "Die Lorelei" (based on the German folk song about a mermaid, combing her hair at the top of a cliff alongside a particularly perilous bend in the Rhine, who lures sailors to shipwreck and death when they are mesmerized by her beauty and by her song). After I shared the dream with the poetry workshop, the girl from home said she had a book for me to read and brought me a copy of *The Hero with a Thousand Faces,* and then pointed out a passage on the devouring goddess!

It took me many years to recognize the motifs of the threshold crossing in my dream and the presence of Aphrodite, goddess of love, born from the bloody whirlpool of blood and foam stirred up by her father's severed genitals. And I know now I myself was the shipwrecked sailor, having lost my mother to suicide and two dear friends to drugs before I turned twenty-five, and without a clue about my future.

A few months after sharing *The Hero* with me, the same girl gave me a flyer from the Mann Ranch in California announcing a two-week trip to Northern France to study the Arthurian Romances of the Middle Ages with Joseph Campbell. I signed up, devoured *The Masks of God: Creative Mythology (vol. 4)* and, an ignorant twenty-six-year-old, one early September autumn afternoon found myself sitting on a bus beside Joseph Campbell, hearing him tell the story of climbing up the belfry at Chartres Cathedral to ring the bells, when he was twenty-six, and identifying every single figure in the Bible in the stained glass and sculpture of that great church. When I walked through the Royal Portal the next morning and moved towards the great octagonal labyrinth on the pavement of the nave, the organist burst into a rehearsal of Bach's famous Toccata—it seemed just for me! All the stones in the church trembled, as if they were about to collapse.

The visit to Chartres came near the end of a really terrific week, which had included visits to Rouen, Amiens, Mt. St. Michel, the standing stones of Carnac, the medieval forests of Brittany, the chateaux country of the Loire River Valley, and then on to Paris. On

160

the bus from the Loire River into Chartres at twilight, Campbell beamed with delight in his window seat beside me, looking out at a host of chateaux entirely invisible to me: he had piercing blue eyes and knew the terrain well—where to look beneath a cluster of trees, or behind a tiny copse in the distance, for the noble relics of the Middle Ages.

We'd had lunch on the grounds of one of the chateaux earlier in the day, sitting beside the still pool that surrounded the beautiful building, which was perfectly reflected on the surface of the water: spires, towers, turrets, crenellations, copes, and barbicans—all perfectly replicated, though pointing downwards, in the serene mirror of the pool's surface. The castle shimmered, above and below the waterline, a dazzling white surrounded by a bevy of immemorial oaks.

It was as if we had stepped through a hole in the hedge into another world or as if we had passed through a door of glass into the mysterious chambers of Glastonbury Abbey, where Arthur and his court danced the Nine Men's Morris.

Our group had stopped earlier in a little pub in the woods of Brittany to have a cup of cider, some cheese, and to enjoy the fine hospitality of our perfectly darling old French host, a diminutive white-haired dwarf with a mystical sense of humor. After several glasses of cider, we strolled down the long path outside the pub, which led into the woods where Vivian had beguiled Merlin—a picture of which our host had carved into the cedar panels of his bar. Stopping beneath a tremendous flowering hawthorn, the old man said to me:

"Il y'a beaucoup de choses qui n'existent pas!" (There are many things which don't exist!)

Deep inside the woods where our group walked after lunch, we all sat down in a circle, sitting on logs and fallen tree trunks amidst the briars and a scattering of Amanita muscaria mushrooms.

"Don't eat those," Campbell said, "or we'll never get to Paris!"

He then told the story of Merlin's marriage.

At the end of his life, the old man fell in love with Vivian the sorceress (also known as Morgan la Fey), who coaxed his magic spells out of him, then used them to imprison the old wizard in a tower of white thorns, in which he remains eternally invisible. Only the sound of his voice—whispering with the wind blowing gently through the trees of the vast forest—comes to those knights who wander through the forests of Broceliande in quest of love, or the Holy Grail.

As Campbell finished his story, with hounds bellowing in the distance, the sun broke free from the mist, and its shafts penetrated the tall oak trees surrounding our silent, spellbound little group. It continued to shine on the shimmering surface of the little pond where we had lunch, Campbell leaning against a standing stone on the shore, with the Lady of the Lake retrieving Excalibur in the water behind him: I imagined I saw her hand extended from beneath the rippling surface, waving the dazzling steel three times in the air before returning to the depths.

The next day, we drove on to visit Mt. St. Michel, staying at a little hotel down the road where Eisenhower had set up offices after the Normandy invasion—whose beaches we had driven by that day. In Rouen, I saw where machine guns had gouged gaping holes in the Cathedral, and an old woman took me into her burned-out basement to thank me for liberating France!

I conveyed her gratitude to my father.

In the peaceful hotel near Mt. St. Michel, Campbell sat quietly in a corner after breakfast before his slide-illustrated lecture, for which he said he was "composing his images." The evening before, a few of us had gone out after dinner to see the Mount at night, rising mysteriously above the dark swirl of the treacherous tides, pinnacle and archangel invisible in the darkness above. We drove together with a National Geographic photographer working on a story there and walked up along the cobbled streets of the village to the colossal arch leading into the monastery and cathedral.

I leaned back against the stone barricades to gaze up at the huge, fluted arches supporting the massive weight of the monastery, which eerily dissolved into the intangible darkness of the endless night above.

"It's the impenetrable inner Self," Fred whispered to me, as I stood with thighs trembling in the wind.

Fred was a bandy-legged, feisty little Australian analyst—with a laugh like a gattling gun—who had received his Jungian calling from a hallucinatory crow, which sat on his right thigh for years, refusing to fly away until he began his analysis! (Do you know the Norse myth of the two ravens, named Thought and Memory, perched on Wotan's shoulders?)

My trembling returned later in Paris, when a small group of us walked over to Notre Dame and then down by the river after a lengthy dinner (with lots of wine). The sight of the powerful, vaulted nave and apse of the Cathedral, seen from the Seine below, with the flurry of flying arches supporting the weight, overwhelmed me. The trembling didn't stop until one of our companions, an older woman who ran a philanthropic foundation in California, simply melted on the stone steps climbing up from the embankment: she'd had far too much wine!

After that marvelous trip to France, followed by trips with Campbell to Egypt and Kenya and seminars at the Open Eye in New York, I decided to go to graduate school in Comparative Literature and set off across the country to Claremont Graduate school in California—where I stayed for seven years, like Hans Castorp trapped on the Magic Mountain in Thomas Mann's great novel. In the very first year, 1980 I think it was, I got a flyer from the leader of a Jungian dream group I was in about a week-long seminar with Campbell at Casa Maria, down the road from Montecito.

I signed up.

During one incredible week, I watched completely amazed as Campbell, then I think in his late seventies, lectured all day long and then into the evening.. In another week at the San Francisco Jung Institute, he went through all of Joyce and Mann from dawn to dusk, with unflagging delight. He would get up in the morning, speak through to lunch, speak all afternoon to dinnertime, and then pick up the ball for a couple of hours after dinner. And he kept it up for a solid week. That kind of stamina at that age, communicating a stunning breadth and detail of information with the kind of grace the Italians call *sprezzatura* (making a difficult task look easy), has been the inspiration of my teaching career.

"It's the heart," Campbell told me while standing in an airport in Nairobi. He had kept fit for many years swimming laps at the New York Athletic Club. "It's the heart."

Words I will always remember, and be grateful for having heard.

After that week at Casa Maria, I continued to drive up from Claremont throughout the course of graduate studies to hear Campbell and then James Hillman, both of whose works I combined to lay the foundation for my dissertation and the seven or so books that came afterwards. I knew I wanted to write about myth and modernist literature and had a vague focus on the model of the hero's journey. Hillman's *Dream and the Underworld* helped me specify the myth as the descent to the underworld and to focus on the revelation of those archetypal forms that govern and shape life, revealed at the climax of

163

the descent—I call these images *necrotypes*, combining the words *archetype* and *nekyia*, Homeric Greek for the descent into Hades.

At a time when Derrida, Lacan, deconstructionism, and post-structuralism were all the rage, and Campbell and Jung were both "discredited," I stuck to my guns, proud to be able to state my thesis topic in two sentences, and followed my bliss, teaching and publishing articles and books about the descent to the underworld in literature from antiquity to postmodernism.

Still, it is amazing that I survived and, forced to move to Switzerland for my first job, managed to get work in my field where there was very little to be found. When I came back after two years of teaching at Franklin College in Lugano, I turned on the television at my step-grandparents summer home on Fire Island and watched spellbound (and naked) as Bill Moyers got Campbell to tell the story about the day he rang the bells of Chartres. Shortly after the series, Campbell died in Hawaii, the land beyond the waves.

I imagine him, at the moment of his heart attack, hearing the crack of a pistol shot at the beginning of a relay race, on the track at Columbia, his spirit taking flight in a long and beautiful run while his body falls to the floor.

Shortly after his death, I had a dream about him.

In the dream, I was walking down one of the avenues in New York City. When I turned off onto a side street, I came to a nondescript doorway with no address and nothing written above it. On a whim, I walked up the dark stairway to an empty room on the upper floor, where I sat down with Joseph Campbell. He had a bell jar in his hand, a kind of alchemical beaker, hermetically sealed. A vaporous mist hovered over some dirt in the bottom of the jar into which we both gazed, Campbell with that marvelous smile of delight that so often illuminated his features. As we looked into the jar, the mist slowly swirled around and became animated with the delicate colors of the rainbow. Campbell pointed to the rainbow—the *Cauda pavonis*, or peacock's tail of the alchemical marriage—and I was led to see in it the emergence of life from the mysterious, invisible forces of the universe, into which the colorful apparition would return at the end of the cycle, evaporated into thin air like a dream.

As we watched the phosphorescent mist swirl above the handful of earth at the bottom of the beaker, a tiny couple slowly became visible, two faerie children with nearly transparent bodies of light. They were joined at the waist, like Siamese twins, by a tiny incision. Again, I was led to understand, with no words passing between us, that this was an alchemical marriage, herald of the new life that was just then beginning for me.

I spent the next twenty years or so exploring and teaching the myth of the descent to the underworld in literature, film, and painting, with a focus on the modernist movements of the twentieth century. Writing those eight books has been the joy of my life—Campbell taught me to follow my bliss, and I did.

But in the dreadful year of 2003 to 2004, the foundation of my life collapsed. At the age of 54, almost overnight, I divorced. After years of being emotionally and verbally abused, I was attacked one night, threatened with a hammer and kitchen knife, deep gouges scratched into my neck and shoulders.

The next day, all the antiques in the garage were smashed to pieces, along with my two very precious guitars.

Thank God she left, after my daughter called the police for help.

Then my children left home to go to college.

I was completely alone.

As necessary as the divorce had been (I see it now as a sacrament, salvation for people who lose themselves in relationships that don't work), it was still the emptiest, most god-awfully haunted nest anyone at midlife could endure.

So I fell into a deep depression, and made the mistake of going to a doctor to get an antidepressant called Paxil. If I wasn't sick before I took the medicine, I certainly was afterwards. The effects were devastating. I have never been so paranoid, so crippled by dread and anxiety, in my entire life. I fell into the underworld I had been writing about for twenty years.

I stopped exercising.

I stopped eating.

I couldn't get out of bed.

For nearly six months.

One morning, the muscles in my calves snapped from long disuse.

I lost everything, took a leave of absence, and saw no way out of the abyss. I mean no way. I imagined both myself and my dear children homeless and exposed to the ruthless forces of Mother Nature in Texas: tornadoes, hailstorms, torrential rain, scorching heat.

Then, two amazing things happened to show me the way out of

the inferno.

First, a woman I may as well call Ariadne came into my life, months after the divorce. I fell deeply in love. She helped me find my way out of the labyrinth—not by babying or nursing me but by forcing me to stand on my own two feet and to become a man for the first time in my life.

Then she invited me to go to Hawaii with her, where she was presenting a paper at a conference. The first thing we did, right off the airplane, was to visit Joseph Campbell's grave in the family plot of a cemetery just north of Honolulu. Ari found the grave in the Erdman family plot. It was a small stone marked *Joseph Campbell,* already overgrown with grass and nearly illegible.

"He's not here," I thought. "He's everywhere." Like Merlin, invisibly sleeping in his tower of flowering hawthorns.

I knelt to put two flowers on the stone and then looked up at the towering slender palms, waving in the wind blowing up from Waikiki (where Campbell had been taught to surf by the Duke). The late afternoon sunlight was dazzling, radiant, and tender. When I turned away to look towards the mountains, I saw a double rainbow in the mist, appearing and disappearing in an uncanny rhythm.

It was a really beautiful moment.

But I hadn't fully recovered from my illness and when we came back from the trip, Ari backed away. Too much pressure, I know, nursing a sick man back to health. I had to let her go and then crawl back towards the coffin.

Then came the second miracle.

In the depths of my despair—in the belly of the whale, at the bottom of the abyss—I got a call from Patrick Mahaffey, director of the Mythological Studies Program at Pacifica Graduate Institute.

"Would you like to teach a course on the Grail legends next year?" he asked.

"Sure," I said.

Then I hung up the phone quickly so I wouldn't have to say anything more, and crawled back into my coffin.

Where I stayed right up until Christmas.

Then, by some miracle I still don't fully understand—the spirit has unfathomable mysteries of its own—I climbed out of the grave, stopped taking the Paxil, and began to walk again—in the early hours of the dawn, when no one could see me—putting one foot in front of the other, step by step.

I watched the crescent of the waning moon sink, with the ghost of the full moon in her lap: a celestial Pièta.

Then I jogged for a lap.

Then another.

Then I got back on the bike.

And slowly, piece by piece, I put Humpty Dumpty back together.

Then, gathering all the courage I could muster, I went back to work—that first day was one of the hardest days of my life, made so touchingly easier by loving friends and understanding colleagues. I started helping my kids again, and, most important of all, I recovered the lost thread of my love for Ariadne.

She wouldn't want me to say so, but without her I wouldn't have made it. At least not in the way I have—so very, very blessed by her love as I have been.

And so, after twenty years of writing about the underworld and one terrible year spent in its uttermost depths, I find myself continuing to follow my bliss, teaching the Grail legends and other mythologies at Pacifica.

And, when it comes to passages in the tales about knights healed from their wounds and/or madness by an ointment provided by The Three Mary's (Lancelot) or Morgan the Wise (Yvain) or Orgeluse (Gawain), I teach them with soul, knowing more than I can say, but perhaps what the world well knows:

A woman's love can bring a man back from any grave he may have dug for himself, or been pushed into.

"Phall if you will, but rise you must," is the way Joyce puts it in *Finnegans Wake*.[2] Joseph Campbell puts it this way: "At the bottom of the abyss comes the voice of salvation. The black moment is the moment when the real message of transformation is going to come. At the darkest moment comes the light."

Notes

[1] Joseph Campbell, *The Masks of God: Creative Mythology* (London: Souvenir Press, 1968), 375.
[2] James Joyce, *Finnegans Wake* (New York: Viking Press, 1939).

UNDER THE HELMET

Mary Aswell Doll

Youth demands images for its imagination and for forming its memory.
~Giambattista Vico

When students enter their first day of a ten-week course on World Mythology, the room is dark. On a large screen they see an illustration of a dragon drawn by artist Ciruelo Cabral for a calendar. It is January. The January image on the calendar is of a very large, leather-winged creature circling over a small dragon-caller below, who in turn stands in the center of a winding path that could as well be a labyrinth. The students, seated in a big circle, are quiet, not so much because they are in awe of the dragon spirit looming in front of them as a projected image but because it is eight in the morning, trouble for art students used to staying up late. They are on this first day, to use their favorite word, *even* tired: eyes lidded, faces carefully composed. I ask them to stand with me so we can stretch. They do. I take long strides going this way and that around the room and ask them to do the same. Some do. The day has begun, the scene set. We are in a special world, having crossed the threshold to await the trials ahead.

I call roll. It is not the usual roll call. It is more a calling forth of names. I give every name its due and look at the responder. Later, I explain that naming is one form of creating, that without a name there can be no identity. Students are probably familiar with God's calling forth light and dark and Adam's naming every living creature: "the cattle, the fowl of the air, and every beast of the field."[1] Students will do the same. In their first act of creation, they will name the group they have randomly formed. Now the room fills with Pitys, The Furies, Aeolus, Yanwang, Chango, Gogo, Icarus, Inktomi, Moloch; Loup Garrou, Nkuba, Bacchus, Soma. We have expanded our company.

I tell each group to call forth a pair of opposites and shout out the pair, using the word "versus" to distinguish one from the other. The air rings with dark versus light, man versus woman, nature versus human, death versus life. Silence. I let the versuses settle. The students seem pleased; they understand dichotomy.

"Now," I instruct, "you are to call out the same pair of opposites, but this time use the word 'and' and emphasize the 'and.'" The air stirs with dark and light, man and woman, nature and human, death and life. Silence. They have not emphasized "and" enough. They must do the exercise again. Still not enough "and." They do the calling again, each time urging the "and" to get louder. I am pleased; the students seem confused with fusing. Our foray into the world of mythology has begun. We are awakened.

It has taken me four tries with this course, over four years, to achieve a level in which I feel I can offer the students an experience. The first time I taught this course, I stumbled over the plots of stories, constructed little charts, worried about the facts and differences among the archetypes, gave quizzes. I was not having a good time. My emphasis was all wrong: I thought I should be instructing. Now my emphasis is entirely different, partly because I am more familiar with the material, have a better set of texts, and (this is important) am older. I have come into my cronehood and know that wisdom cannot be taught, but offering an experience can be mind-changing. The material is grand; I will never crack all its codes. But I have taken off the helmet and wish the same for my students.

My emphasis is different now, too, because I feel urgency about the "matter" of the material. We are not just talking here about good stories, although we certainly are doing that. Instead, we are talking about a fundamental way of viewing the cosmos, the Earth, and human relationships therein. Today's science is yesterday's myth: fractals, subatomic physics, and chaos theory are (simply) new terms and patterns for the webs and whorls of ancient goddess cultures. A fundamental unity exists among all matter, myth and science would agree. The Gaia hypothesis, suggested by James Lovelock,[2] proclaims that Earth is not inert, to be dominated by God or Adam or man; rather, Earth is a complex organic living system involving biosphere, atmosphere, oceans, and soil. New science is old myth. Astonishing!

To return to a study of the goddess is to risk upsetting some students, female and male alike, who are comfortable with our patriarchal culture and its still-strong Judeo-Christian bias. Today one can hardly escape images of women anchors on cable television made to look chirpy, thin, and nonoffensive, giving us the "news" of the day with no mention whatsoever of what is really happening on Earth, to Earth. The patriarchy has helmeted women, kept them down. But teaching is a subversive act, I have come to believe, that requires reverence for the little word "and" if we are to bring back into consciousness a mythic sense of balance. A removal of the helmet allows the snake, precursor of the dragon, to be seen. Let me explain.

For her final project a quiet student, whose last name is Boo, chooses to illustrate a little known (to me) story connected with Athena. Familiar is the picture of gray-eyed Athena with helmet and shield, identified as the warrior virgin daughter of Zeus. Familiar too is the description of that shield, containing Medusa's head wrapped with snakes. Less familiar is Erichthonius, whom Athena carried in a basket. He was the serpent-child born of the sperm Hephaestus spilled onto Athena's leg, which was wiped off by her onto the ground, Gaia's womb. Gaia gives the snake-child to Athena, presumably the creature's rightful mother, who hands off the child in a basket to the daughters of King Cecrops, himself part-man, part-snake. When the daughters can't resist looking inside the basket, against the goddess's prohibition, they are so appalled by what they see that they throw themselves over a cliff to their deaths.

I can't get my mind around this strange little story, never having seen a portrayal of Athena with a basket. That is, until Ms. Boo draws three pictures. I am almost as enthralled with her drawings, so primitive and stark, as I am by what must have captured this quiet student's mind. In one triptych are the Athena panel with the basket containing the snake-child, another panel showing King Cecrops in his man-snake appearance, and a third panel portraying a toothless Erichthonius smiling inside the basket. Three in one. Then my mind circles around the chthonics hidden inside the name Erichthonius: in name and story Athena is intimately connected with snakes, but in a hidden way. Why does the Athena of classical art portray such a different, more cleansed and mighty image of the goddess? And why do the daughters of a snake-human father act with such fear when seeing a creature so like their father?

The answer, in retrospect, is obvious. Of course! The helmeted Athena casts a virginal image established during the patriarchal sky religion of classical times and gleaned from the writings of Hesiod, Pindar, and Apollodorus. She is a male construction of the new order. Even the first text I used in this course, written by a well-respected Jungian male scholar, makes scant mention of this other, chthonic aspect of Athena, as if he disregarded or did not know about Erichthonius (there is no mention of him in the text). The only fact that is mentioned is that Athena "probably" originated as a fertility patroness of the Minoan rulers.[3] Note how dry a "fact" sounds. But there is no "probably" about it! As early (ca. 520 B.C.E) statues depict her, Athena is a wild and awesome goddess (not a patroness) whose head is garlanded in snakes and whose garment is fringed with snakes and whose left hand firmly holds the head of a snake. Snake, in the early goddess culture, is symbolic—not literal. The symbol of the goddess holding a snake or being associated with the snake is symbolic of the "andness" of the cycle of life and death, over which the ancient fertility goddesses ruled. With its skin-shedding, the snake symbolizes regeneration, much as does the moon's waning and waxing. So, far from being a citified patroness complete with helmet and shield, Athena once held powers that caused her image to be truly awe-full rather than merely mighty.

But to read the image for its symbolic quality—*that* is the lifelong task of the student of myth. I confess that I teach that which I struggle to understand and reading symbols is difficult for me, since I tend to be a literal-minded helmet wearer. But my students have always pointed the way and teach me much. Ms. Boo's drawings deconstruct Athena's classical depiction, enabling me to read her images with both eyes open. And to return to those daughters hurling themselves over the cliff: I suggest that that little nugget inside the little story about the serpent-child, inside the little basket (many coilings around the secret), is meant to keep the chthonic connection of Athena hidden in plain sight. Those who see the image literally as "monster" fall and die; they fail to read beneath the surface of the thing.

Now, I step back out of this class. I have a half-hour lunch break, enough time for me to adjust my mind, catch my breath, and leap forward a few centuries. I enter my second course of the quarter, "The Absurdist Imagination," a course I devised in which we read in rounds

Gertrude Stein, playact Ionesco and Beckett, and view Beckett's *Footfalls* on a DVD. The classroom remains in a circle for the round readings, with my role as conductor in the center, waving a ruler to the rhythms of repeated words and pointing to voices high and low for change and mood. The students either love or hate Gertrude Stein (mostly hate). They take her childlike simplicities to be nothing more than childish, not catching the dimension of meanings layered in her deliberate repeatings. And my! how Gertrude loves to play with the word "things, " as in *something, anything;* or *some thing, any thing;* and how her "simple things" turn with each variation of the pattern: "It is a simple thing to be quite certain that there are kinds in men and women. It is a simple thing and then not any one has any worrying to be doing about any one being any one. It is a simple thing to be quite certain that each one is one being a kind of them. . . ."[4] Fragments like this, and so many others, are like bell ringings, resonances. Stein is being ironic, teasing us about our simplistic judgments, our ready reach for labeling, our need, somehow, to reduce especially our notion of gender. What is a man, a woman, anyhow? How simple, though, to accept that there are "kinds" of men, "kinds" of women that elude classification! Any "one" can be many "things."

In this class my helmet becomes a repository for simple things, so I ask my students as they work their way through the readings to use their heads likewise. Let us listen and laugh, I suggest—not laugh "at" but "with"—in the simple delight of hearing language play its sounds for us in our ears. "The lower the order of mental activity the better the company."[5] Beckett urges a return to a more open mind: less thinking, more listening; less figuring out, more letting figures in.

For the playacting, we move the chairs around: some in rows, some back-to-back, some in the front, some in the back. Students become who they are not, become someone else for a change, possibly become the someone elses who inhabit their interiority, at least for a while. I read with them, taking part, playing roles: all this so as to cultivate the gracious, difficult work of memory. How, I ask, do these writers and playwrights urge us *out* of ourselves so that we can occupy ourselves more deeply? How do these wisps of stories—not chronologically told, certainly not logically arranged—enable us to connect with the vigorous presences of our pasts? The final project, an absurdist autobiography, asks these questions.

Beckett's work seems to be formative for many students. Viewing the film *Footfalls* is really a viewing of sound. (Again, sound. I theorize that part of the difficulty with the reductive insistence of our culture, which so loves the word "basically," is that we are too sight-oriented. Everything needs to be on the surface; everything needs to be basic.) With Beckett's play, we hear the sound May's feet make as she wheels and turns in elliptics. We see her distress but intuit it more by the rhythmic tread of her feet and by the long pauses between her words than by plot or speech. How faint the feet fall! For my leg-jigglers in class, I wonder how they would take the eighteen or so minutes of viewing sound and silence, with very little dialogue. Some are mesmerized. Some are resistant, at first. I liken the experience to watching Buddhist monks create a mandala, sand drop by sand drop, small sounds serving to emphasize silence. Beckett's ghostly actress on the screen is hardly real, more like a Demeter figure searching in distress for a lost part of herself. Her words, the situation, the scraps of dialogue are allusive, indirect, and dislocated. Those are the qualities I ask my students to work toward for their final project, a series of memory pieces re-collected.

We read *Company*, what I have termed Beckett's autobiography. Here are the same kinds of allusiveness, indirection, and dislocation as seen/heard in *Footfalls*. It is a memory piece, an example of what the students are to produce. Their first drafts are too emotional, too full of personality, too literal. Work for distance, I suggest. Avoid sentiment. Fill your head with images, not plots. Work with rhythms. Use the second-person pronoun. Use refrain.

These are difficult instructions. I think back to my own undergraduate years, wondering whether I could do this assignment with the degree of sophistication that Lavar and Stephanie manage:

> In kindergarten, you cried. You were four. In college, did you cry? You were twenty-four. . . . You wanted to be a veterinarian. You always loved animals, what went wrong? There was always a pencil and paper around. Besides, your uncles drew; they were your role models. You draw, and your younger cousins all draw. You are their role model. During the summer months, you always begged for money to purchase rubber bands. With rubber bands you made sling shots. With sling shots you hunted, you killed. Don't you remember?

You forgot about your tadpole farm, you left them to die, to decay, and to disappear. Birds will always be birds. They will forever dominate the skies. You gave your birds away. They flew away. You grew tired of them and they grew tired of you. They are now wild, no more dependent, they miss you. You destroyed your shells, you regret it, they soothed your mind. Now you paint them, people cherish them, you let go of them, it's   your job; you love it, you live it, you breathe it, you dream it, it's a game; who killed it?. . . .

You continue.

In his artist statement, Lavar writes about the influence Beckett has on his writing this piece—"Clippings," he calls it. He comments that he wants to write as if someone were dictating his life to him. He wants to convey Beckett's sense of long suffering. Hearing him read these clippings in his Caribbean accent is, the class agrees, moving.

Stephanie also catches a sense of how it is to live a life aware of the multitudinous things and voices that fill one's head. She catches—remarkably, I think—the sense of the child put into a world where contradiction is not at all a problem. A child's mind ebbs and flows between the opposites naturally. She titles her piece "A One Year Old Amongst the Gypsies":

You are aware of them. They are not very far but their presence is distant. A body breezes by you. Close then far. Not very far, no. . . . not very   close. Present and not very far. An airy skirt brushed against you. It feels like nothing. It feels wonderful and unremarkable. You sit on the concrete pavilion floor amongst the picnic tables. You are touched in passing. It feels wonderful. It is unremarkable. How remarkable it was. You haven't forgotten, you never think of it. . . .

You are content on your own, outside of their tall world. You cling to one object. One token among many. You ignore the others. You cling to that one. You open and close it. It was meant for hands like yours, fingers like yours. It is small and it gets smaller and smaller. She splits down the middle. She splits down the middle and inside her there is another. She splits down the middle and inside her, another. Smaller and smaller, over and over, they fit inside one another, all these same faces inside the

175

same face. Time passes. You see and you look. They are not very far but their presence is distant. You are content on your own. The scent of home is around you. You are illuminated and it is dark. Time passes. . . .

I have nothing left to say, wanting my students' voices to resonate. I am grateful to Lavar and Stephanie and Ms. Boo. During an intense ten-week quarter they stand out in my mind as ones who do more than I could have done at their age. I will remember them as they help me re-member my teaching. My wish is that all our classrooms be a place where the someones in our charge find their own some ones under the helmet.

Notes

[1] Gen. 2: 20.
[2] James Lovelock, *Gaia: A New Look at Life on Earth* (New York: Oxford University Press, 1979).
[3] David Adams Leeming, *The World of Myth* (New York: Oxford University Press, 1990), 103.
[4] Gertrude Stein, *Matisse, Picasso and Gertrude Stein. With Two Shorter Stories* (Minneola, New York: Dover, 2000), 23.
[5] Samuel Beckett, *Company* (New York: Grove, 1980), 12.

TEACHING AS MOTHERING THE SOUL

Rosemarie Anderson

Someday, maybe, I may be brave enough to start class on the first
day by singing, in my husky alto voice,
"I don't know why I love you like I do. I don't know why, I just do."[1]

To teach is to mother the soul in another. In acts of love formed of
soft tissue and hard bones, teachers mother what is possible in others.
Sometimes, the soft tissue of teaching is tender, supple, and expansive.
Sometimes, the hard bones enact discipline, planning, and timeliness.
Whether soft or hard, mothering the soul tenders what is like oneself
and, especially, what is unlike oneself in another. In order to teach well,
a teacher must also learn to take care of herself. Such a teacher is a
master.

Thirty years ago, as a twenty-nine-year-old assistant professor, I
had a low-grade fever that continued for weeks. I arrived at my two
sections of Introductory Psychology filled with bright-eyed freshman
and sophomores and wondered whether I had enough energy to make
it through the hour. I did not have my usual peppy energy to keep a
class lively. So I decided to love them instead. I gave my prepared
lectures, but my style was sweeter and more tender. At the end of the
course, my students did as well on their multiple-choice exams as
previous students had, but my teaching reviews took the top off the
scale. I am a loquacious and naturally gifted teacher, but that semester
my reviews were better than they had ever been.

A Litany for Teaching, Asking for Blessing

This essay is a litany dedicated to mothering the soul of students through acts of love that further what is possible in others. As I have been an Episcopal priest since 1986 and a transpersonal researcher and teacher since the early 1990s, I am accustomed to praying in public settings and leading meditations on all manner of esoteric topics. Therefore, I write this chapter as a litany, sounded aloud in a set of prayers sent out into the universe in a collective voice. We ask for blessing that the values we hold dear are set into action in our teaching endeavors. I lean my heart forward toward you as we pray together.

Each short prayer and response below is followed by a brief commentary about mothering the soul in teaching. The reader's congregational responses are in *italics*. Let us begin.

Let us pray. Let our meditations soar.

Fill my heart with compassion for my students and the world. Each day as I begin teaching may I be blessed that whatever I do be clothed in kindness—even when I am not feeling so very kind myself.

Goodness of creation, listen to me!

All teachers get angry at their students. Anyone who has taught for a while knows that there are moments when you want to rip your students from tip-top to toe.

Only yesterday, a student e-mailed me asking exactly when she could expect a response on her dissertation proposal. I felt ordered around and forced into a corner amid my own deadlines. Her e-mail request tore at my Scandinavian work ethic, and I felt a little crazy. I e-mailed back a succinct and probably testy response telling her that I was behind schedule because I had been ill. Somehow, I had expected more from her—that she would see me as a person with exigencies of my own. Only days later did I feel compassion for her vulnerability as a young woman who was writing a dissertation and trying to get her career moving forward with an infant in tow. My frazzled response required more of me and more from her; more compassion from both of us for each other. However badly we handled our e-mail exchange, the conversation changed us both. Now we are kinder and more honest with one another.

Instill in me the spaciousness and expanse that fills the starry skies at night. May my ordinary acts be touched by possibilities untold and beyond my knowing so students may discover that learning is fun and not just memorization, drill, and work.

Night sky and stars, fill me with wonder.

Etymologically, to be enthusiastic is to be *en-theo*, to be infused with divine spirit. I always teach best when I turn myself over to wonder. Students catch my enthusiasm. Sometimes, I catch theirs. The winds of enthusiasm purify what is false or inessential, and I speak more from essence—from my soul to theirs. I simply cannot care deeply about a topic without caring deeply about others and the impact of what I am saying and doing on others and the universe around me. So, over time, the jammed-up information stored in memory from reading books and Internet searches is sorted out, prioritized, and purified. What is important stands out clearly from what is not. What is rightful and good identifies itself from what is not.

Enthusiasm is also Eros, passion born of deep desire to know and to relate. Through passion information connects to belonging to others and to a universe that loves. The starry skies at night are not blank or empty: they are filled with immensity, energy, and movement. Impulses born of Eros propel the teacher and her students into relationship with life, both animate and inanimate, with the starry skies. Enthusiasm for knowledge and skill brings us into relationship with the universe, so in time acquiring knowledge and skill becomes a vocation of belonging to the world.

Work in me the gift of silence and solemnity that my quietude may hear the authentic voice of the most unruly students and the silent ones who ask nothing and rarely speak. May their needs be magnified in my ears.

Silence, let me hear.

For many years, I have considered teaching a transformative or spiritual practice because it helps me become a better person. Teaching calls out the best in me. Perhaps like many mothers in the face of the needs of others, I surrender my own minor needs and ego satisfactions; they vanish into thin air. I become both less myself and more myself, because the responsive mode of teaching calls me to improve my character. For me, the surest sign that I am "on target" as a teacher is that I am not forgetting the unruly and silent students in the collective of faces. Over time, what I learn in the art of teaching extends to all my relations. I notice more and am more responsive.

For some of you, the phrase "mothering the soul" might not fit with your way of teaching. Perhaps, spiritual or transpersonal language does not fit your style either. But most of us know what it is to be called into a vocation. The work feels solid, right, or congruent—and often not like work at all. No matter what the technical or logistical difficulty in teaching, there is always joy beneath the turbulence.

May the kindness I feel for others include me, that I may live and teach well. May I renew myself with sleep, delight, and long vacations. May I not forget that in giving to others I must be rested and playful in order to love.

Bounty of nature, renew me.

Working in a service profession, teachers are asked to do more and more . . . and more. By the time my school year ends, my mind, body, and spirit are rarely working well. I feel "on empty" like a car without gas. Even after a delicious night's sleep, I am weary and grumpy. My mind feels like glue. Words usually come easily to me but not now. Morning sunshine beacons. Cool air excites my skin, prompting me outside. The roses demand fertilizer. I sit in my garden and do nothing whatsoever, not even move. I look forward to shopping and errands—a certain sign that I need diversion and mindless activity.

Most teachers I know struggle with what others want of them and their own need for vacations, weekends, and time off. Yet, rest, delight and vacations are necessities, not luxuries. Teachers like me who have introverted personalities may even require abundant quiet time alone to reestablish their physical, emotional, and spiritual energies. Extraverted personalities may rebound more easily—or appear to. Whatever your personality type, take what you need because no one profits from your exhaustion. Once you have mothered your own soul, fly back to the classroom and create your life work anew.

Give me ferocity to tell administrators under constant hierarchical demands of their own that my students need me more than they do. Allow me to set boundaries and limits appropriate to my time, needs, and competencies. Let me not forget that good teaching requires good boundaries within the institutions that I inhabit.

Wind and thunder, make me fierce.

Most organizations and schools are patriarchal and hierarchical in structure. They can also be racist and misogynist structures, too. They are interested in their own survival and will likely outlive those who work in them. While individuals *within* organizations may care about your well-being, institutional structures are incapable of caring—no matter what the institutional rhetoric. These simple facts are always stressful for me to recognize. In my kind-hearted way of working within benevolent organizations (and schools almost always are), I must remind myself again and again to recognize patriarchal structures for what they are. If I take the fact of these structures too personally, I squander my own energy for what is often already harmful and cannot act decisively in order to protect myself and others.

The best you can do as an employee within such structures is to barter your energy, time, and knowledge for what the institution returns to you financially, professionally, and personally. As long as the trade is fair to you and your loved ones, stay. Otherwise, find another job. Even those who stay must defend their time and

181

energy from demands that serve the institution much more than they serve themselves. Be forewarned. Be vigilant. Be fierce.

Hold me in grace that I may hold others in sacred space in teaching and supervision. May this sacred space prompt freedom, expression, and impulses of wonder wherein identities are found and renewed.

Sun at high noon, shine on me and others.

Not long ago, I taught a session on Celtic Spirituality at one of the Institute of Transpersonal Psychology's Global Seminars. Over a hundred students from locations around the world attended my session. My introverted personality was nervous as I always am in front of large groups of people. I wanted to impart to them not just intellectual knowledge but rather the feeling of the ancient Celts. So for an entire day before the session, through focused attention I created sacred space for them and for me as their leader. While creating a PowerPoint presentation of Celtic symbols, I imagined how we would be together. Therefore, when I arrived the next day to give the presentation, the energy field was already set in place. I had only to step into that field of relationship. When the students arrived, they, too, stepped into a field that was already lively and homogeneous—and very Celtic.

From a transpersonal perspective, I had created ritual or drama, a virtual enactment of what I wanted to impart. While teaching that day, I felt fully present. But, my actions arose more from the energetic field I had created than from myself. The students, too, played their parts, responding to the moment. In psychoanalytic language, projection and transference occurred safely within a contained environment, which I held conscientiously for the duration of the session. They projected onto me an authority that is beyond what I know about the ancient Celts. I hope they learned the deeper aspects of what I intuit about the Celts through my embodied enactment. I learned how better to step aside from my ego while teaching and thereby to allow the energy that arises to embody possibility in the students and me. When the session was over, I stepped out of my teacher's role changed by what we had enacted together.

Within sacred space, content being taught and drama enacted tend to merge as separate entities distinct from teacher and students. What is learned arises spontaneously in the moment.

Help me to set my intentions hurling forward into the future. As I create my own destiny, may I inspire my students to live their own destinies. Through my students, may I belong to the future and inspire hope.

Future generations, help me help you.

When William Braud and I wrote *Transpersonal Research Methods for the Social Sciences* in 1997,[2] we set forth an intention to change the scientific paradigm in the human and social sciences. We wanted to play our part in shifting this scientific paradigm through our teaching, research, and writing. We sat together and prayed. We were happy. We imagined what our dissertation students and research colleagues might need from us in order to create a science that inspired compassion for others and the world. Having both been trained as experimental psychologists and having conducted and taught research courses for many years, we knew intimately the benefits and limitations of the scientific paradigm we had inherited from our scientific predecessors. Now working in the field of transpersonal psychology, we knew that the research methods we had learned in graduate school were also inadequate to the task of exploring the "farther reaches of human nature," as Abraham Maslow put it so well. Fully studying the healing dimension of a psychotherapist, studying being "in the zone" among athletes or the experience of *satori* is not possible unless researchers are willing to personally plumb the depths of these experiences themselves. We must know the territory ourselves of what we study.

Initially, we changed the way research is conducted in the field of transpersonal psychology. In meditation, we sent out an impulse into consciousness that our work would resonate with like-minded researchers throughout the human and social sciences.

The impulse was a seed that might find fertile soil amid the research and scholarly activities of others. We would find colleagues and join together. Together we would change the scientific paradigm toward a kinder and more socially responsible science. Now in 2007, as we prepare to write a follow-up book that introduces transpersonal practices such as mindfulness and empathic identification as research skills, we know that science is changing along with us. There are now many impulses changing the scientific paradigm as we have known it. So, again, we are letting our imaginations soar and guide. This time we are like eagles flying high in the air, asking what future generations may want from us.

Awaken in me delight of being in the moment just as it is, both in quietude and well-deserved rest after a hard day's work and at the end of my working life. May I rest in knowing that others are teaching well.

Goodness of creation, bring me contentment.

Living in the moment just as it is is a lifelong spiritual practice. To remember that life is perfect requires in me an inner reserve and knowing that the universe is fundamentally good and spacious and its essence ecstatic. As time passes, I have begun to feel like the ocean. Down deep there is joy. Like waves, emotions ripple only the surface. Everything is perfect just as it is.

Whatever your vocation, all good work deserves rest and contentment. May everyone reading this essay and sounding these prayers feel that their individual efforts are appreciated and sufficient for the day. May you be blessed in all you do for yourself and for your students.

"I don't know why I love you like I do. I don't know why, I just do."

Notes

[1] "I Don't Know Why," lyrics and music by Roy Turk and Fred E. Ahlert, ©1931,

1946.

2 William Braud and Rosemarie Anderson (1998). *Transpersonal Research Methods for the Social Sciences: Honoring Human Experience* (Thousand Oaks, CA: Sage, 1998).

CONTRIBUTOR BIOGRAPHIES

Stephen Aizenstat, Ph.D., is founding president of Pacifica Graduate Institute and a licensed clinical psychologist. His areas of emphasis include depth psychology, dream research, and imaginal and archetypal psychology. His original research centers on a psychodynamic process of "tending the living image," particularly in the context of dream work. He continues to offer seminars throughout the United States, Europe, and Asia, which he has done for over twenty-five years. He is currently working on a new book, *Dream Tending: Teachings for Dream-Centered Life.* Last year he was featured in a film on dream tending by local filmmaker Russ Spencer, shown at the Santa Barbara International Film Festival. He has taught both at the secondary and university levels, most specifically at M.A. and Ph.D. levels of counseling and clinical psychology. Visit www.dreamtending.com.

Claudia Allums, Ph.D., has been a teacher since 1981, teaching high school English and drama in West Virginia; Arlington, Texas; and Addison, Texas. During her career in secondary education, she also served as assistant principal, curriculum coordinator, lead teacher, and department head. After seventeen years in secondary education, she earned a Ph.D. in literature from the University of Dallas in 2002 and taught the undergraduate Literary Tradition course as well as graduate courses in the humanities. She feels blessed to be working at The Dallas Institute of Humanities and Culture, the institution that was her intellectual and spiritual birthplace in 1989, where she has been the associate director and director of the Teachers Academy since the fall of 2004.

Rosemarie Anderson, Ph.D., is a transpersonal psychologist and Episcopal priest. She is currently Core Faculty at the Institute of Transpersonal Psychology (www.itp.edu) and has taught at the University of Nebraska, Lincoln; Wake Forest University; and in the Asian and European divisions of the University of Maryland. Her publications on Transpersonal Psychology—*Embodied Writing; Body Intelligence;* and *Intuitive Inquiry*—are available at www.wellknowingconsulting.org.

Christopher Bache, Ph.D., has been a professor of Religious Studies at Youngstown State University in Ohio for almost three decades and adjunct faculty at the California Institute of Integral Studies. For two years (2000–2002) he was the director of Transformative Learning at the Institute of Noetic Sciences. An award-winning professor, his areas of teaching include Eastern religious thought, transpersonal psychology, consciousness research, and Buddhism. He is the author of three books: *Lifecycles* (1990), *Dark Night, Early Dawn* (2000), and *The Living Classroom* (2008), from which this essay is an excerpt. His writing explores reincarnation, the philosophical implications of nonstates of consciousness, and teaching and the dynamics of collective consciousness. He has been a Vajrayana practitioner for ten years and is the proud father of three grown children.

Edward S. Casey, Ph.D., is Distinguished Professor at the State University of New York at Stony Brook and teaches as well at the New School for Social Research and at Pacifica Graduate Institute, where he is Distinguished Contributing Faculty. He was chair of the Philosophy Department at Stony Brook from 1991–2001. He has also held teaching positions at Yale, Emory, Amherst College, Williams Collage, and the University of California, Santa Barbara.

His books include *Spirit and Soul: Essays in Philosophical Psychology; Imagining; Remembering; Getting Back into Place; Representing Place in Landscape Painting and Maps;* and *Earth-Mapping: Artists Reshaping Landscape.* A new book, *The World at a Glance,* has just appeared. He has edited, with David Miller, a special issue of *Spring Journal* on Philosophy and Psychology. His recent research bears on the role of edge in human experience.

Mary Aswell Doll, Ph.D., earned her doctorate from Syracuse University in Interdisciplinary Studies with three areas of concentration: aesthetics, religious studies, and modern British literature. She has taught at colleges and universities in New York, California, Maryland, Louisiana, and now Georgia, where she teaches in the Liberal Arts Department at Savannah College of Art and Design. She has published chapters and articles on myth, literature, and teaching. Her recent books include *To the Lighthouse and Back: Writings on Teaching and Living* (1995); *Like Letters in Running Water: A Mythopoetics of Curriculum* (2000); and *Triple Takes on Curricular Worlds* (2006). She is currently working on a collection of essays on teaching.

Christine Downing, Ph.D., currently a professor of Mythological Studies at Pacifica Graduate Institute, taught for almost twenty years in the Department of Religious Studies at San Diego State University (a good part of the time as department chair and during the same period as Core Faculty member at the San Diego campus of the California School of Professional Psychology). From 1963 to 1974 she served as a faculty member of the Religion Department at Douglass College of Rutgers University. She has also taught at the Jung Institute in Zürich and lectures frequently to Jungian groups both here and abroad, including at American and European universities. Her undergraduate degree in literature is from Swarthmore College; her Ph.D. in religion and culture is from Drew University. Her books include *The Goddess; Journey Through Menopause; Psyche's Sisters; Myths and Mysteries of Same-Sex Love; Mirrors of the Self; Women's Mysteries; Gods In Our Midst; The Long Journey Home; The Luxury of Afterwards; Preludes;* and *Gleanings.*

Elizabeth Fergus-Jean, M.F.A., Ph.D., is a visual artist and educator. She teaches in the Liberal Arts and Media Studies departments at Columbus College of Art and Design, and was a founding faculty member of the M.A. in Humanities, Mythology and Education program at Pacifica Graduate Institute. She exhibits her artwork nationally, and it has appeared on the covers of eleven books and international journals in the past several years.

Nancy Treadway Galindo, Ph.D., has worked as an educational consultant, community college instructor, assistant director of a college learning center, and a leader of public seminars. She holds an M.S. in Educational Psychology and a Ph.D. in Depth Psychology. Her teaching experience includes college courses in psychology, communication, personal development, and dream work. She recently presented a workshop on scholarly writing at Pacifica Graduate Institute. She conducts women's support groups and dream groups as well as consults in private dream work. She has published *Tending the Living Dream Image: A Phenomenological Study.*

Robin L. Gordon, Ph.D., is the director of the Secondary Teacher Preparation Program at Mount St. Mary's College. She began her career as a secondary science teacher in both public and private schools in Southern California. She then completed a Ph.D. in Education at Claremont Graduate University and a second Ph.D. in Depth Psychology at Pacifica Graduate Institute. Her area of research is multidisciplinary. She is writing about classroom strategies that go beyond traditional teaching methods, such as using dialogue and story to help secondary students achieve more depth in their studies. She is also writing a book on women alchemists that crosses the fields of women's studies, history of science, and depth psychology. See her website at www.womenalchemists.com.

Matthew Green, Ph.D., has worked in education for over twenty years. For fifteen years, he served as director and principal teacher of a Study Abroad program for the School for International Training, primarily in Toulouse, France. All the while he was teaching abroad, he wondered how the learning that he saw his students experience, which naturally engaged the imagination and the heart, might be brought to schools "at home." Since 2002, he has been director of Community Education at Cuesta College in San Luis Obispo, CA. He has a Ph.D. in Depth Psychology from Pacifica Graduate Institute.

James Hillman, Ph.D., is a world-renowned psychologist of imagination and culture. For the past five decades he has been writing and speaking on the imagination that underpins culture and psyche. Founder of Archetypal Psychology and the author of dozens of books and articles, including *Re-Visioning Psychology, A Terrible Love of War, The Soul's Code,* and *The Force of Character,* he has received many honors, including the Medal of the Presidency of the Italian Republic. He has held distinguished lectureships at Yale, Princeton, The University of Dallas, and Pacifica Graduate Institute, among others. For over a decade he was director of the Jung Psychoanalytic Institute in Zurich.

Currently *The Uniform Edition of The Writings of James Hillman* is being published in conjunction with The Dallas Institute Publications under the direction of Dr. Joanne H. Stroud at The Dallas Institute of Humanities and Culture, with additional support from The Feitel Foundation in New Orleans; Pacifica Graduate Institute in Carpinteria, California; and the Joseph Campbell Archives and Library in Carpinteria. This essay was originally published as part of Chapter 41, "City, Soul, and Myth," in *City and Soul,* edited by Robert J. Leaver as Volume 2 of *The Uniform Edition of the Writings of James Hillman* (pp. 394–99). It is reprinted here with the generous permission of James Hillman.

Betty McEady, Ed.D., fascinated by depth psychology and what it can contribute to teaching and learning processes, interrupted her university teaching career to study this at Pacifica Graduate Institute. Her teaching itinerary began in 1966 in secondary schools in Florida, Georgia, and eventually California. Combining a teaching career and advanced studies in teaching, she completed an Ed.D. in Curriculum and Instruction/Language Arts and Literacy at the University of San Francisco in 1982. This launched her twenty-five-year career in teacher education in the California State University system. She was a cofounding faculty and educational leader at CSU, Monterey Bay, from 1995 to 2007. Her professional activity and scholarship areas include: teacher education; literacy development; curriculum and instructional design; multicultural education; outcomes-based education; and best practices in teaching, learning, and assessment. Now, in addition to her studies at Pacifica, she resides in Portland, Oregon and teaches part-time at Portland State University.

Ruth Meyer, Ph.D., was one of the first female undergraduates to be admitted to Corpus Christi College at the University of Oxford in 1979. She studied and taught history in England and Spain for ten years before discovering Carl Jung. She is a pioneer in Jungian psychohistory. Her book, *Clio's Circle: Entering the Imaginal World of Historians,* is published by Spring Journal. It examines the role of dreams and visions of historians as a missing link in the process of writing history. She has been teaching history for a total of twenty-two years, and she currently teaches world history at a college preparatory school in San Jose, California. She continues to present her research on dreams and history at workshops and conferences.

David L. Miller, Ph.D., is Watson-Ledden Professor of Religion, Emeritus, at Syracuse University and a retired Core Faculty member at Pacifica Graduate Institute. He has also taught at many Jung training institutes, including Zurich, Kyoto, Toronto, New York, Los Angeles, and San Francisco. From 1975 until 1988 he was a member of the Eranos Circle in Ascona, Switzerland, and he lectured there on nine different occasions. He was made an Affiliate Member of the Inter-Regional Society of Jungian Analysts in 2002 and an honorary member of the International Association of Analytical Psychology in 2004. He is the author of six books and more than one hundred articles and book chapters. For more information, see his website at http://web.syr.edu/~dlmiller/.

An earlier and more amplified version of his essay appeared as "Nothing to Teach! No Way to Teach It! Together with the Obligation to Teach! Dilemmas in the Rhetoric of Assessment and Accountability," in *Soundings* 82.1–2 (Spring/Summer 1999): 219–240.

Thomas Moore, Ph.D., is an internationally-known author of works that include *Care of the Soul* and *Soul Mates* as well as *A Blue Fire*, an edited volume on the works of James Hillman.

His wide-ranging teaching assignments include teaching music at the primary and secondary levels. He has also taught religion and depth psychology at the university level for thirteen years at such schools as the University of Windsor, Glassboro State College, and

Southern Methodist University. In addition, he has taught art therapists at Lesley University for four years. He has given workshops and offered lectures worldwide for the past three decades. His interests in alternative forms of education, including homeschooling, the topic of this essay, continue to deepen.

Jennifer Leigh Selig, Ph.D., believes she was born with a piece of chalk in her hand and thus rebels against the move to whiteboards in education, among other less innocuous moves noted in this essay. She taught high school in her native Northern California for sixteen years before her rise (fall?) to higher education in Southern California at Mount St. Mary's College and then Pacifica Graduate Institute, where she currently serves as department chair in the Depth Psychology program. She has published four books, including a gift book for graduates titled *What Now?: Words of Wisdom for Life After Graduation* and a book on everyday spirituality titled *Thinking Outside the Church: 110 Ways to Connect With Your Spiritual Nature*. See her website at www.jenniferleighselig.com

Dennis Patrick Slattery, Ph.D., is currently Core Faculty, Mythological Studies Program at Pacifica Graduate Institute in Carpinteria, California. He has taught for 40 years on elementary, secondary, undergraduate and graduate levels. From 1984-87 he taught teachers the classics of literature in the Dallas Institute of Humanities and Culture's Summer Program for Teachers. He also taught for 6 years at the Fairhope Institute of Humanities and Culture's Summer Program for high school teachers, under the direction of Dr. Larry Allums, current director of The Dallas Institute. He is the author or co-editor of 12 books, among them: *The Idiot: Dostoevsky's Fantastic Prince* (1984); *The Wounded Body: Remembering the Markings of Flesh* (2000); *Grace in the Desert: Awakening to the Gifts of Monastic Life* (2003); with Lionel Corbett, he co-edited *Depth Psychology: Meditations in the Field* (2001) and *Psychology at the Threshold* (2002); with Glen Slater, he co-edited *Varieties of Mythic Experience: Essays on Religion, Psyche and Culture* (2008). He has composed three volumes of poetry: *Casting the Shadows: Selected Poems* (2001); *Just Below the Water Line: Selected Poems* (2004); and *Twisted Sky: Selected Poems* (2007). He offers workshops on Joseph Campbell and personal mythology in Jungian groups and organizations in the United States. He is writing a book on *Riting One's Personal Myth: Joseph Campbell and the Journaling Psyche*.

Evans Lansing Smith, Ph.D., is a professor of English at Midwestern State University and adjunct professor of Mythological Studies at Pacifica Graduate Institute. He has a B.A. from Williams College, an M.A from Antioch International, and a Ph.D. from The Claremont Graduate School. He is the author of nine books and many articles on comparative literature and mythology. In the late 1970s, he traveled with Joseph Campbell on tours of Northern France, Egypt, and Kenya. He has taught at colleges and universities in Switzerland, Maryland, California, and Texas.

www.ingramcontent.com/pod-product-compliance
Lightning Source LLC
Chambersburg PA
CBHW070349090426
42733CB00009B/1342